NEW TESTAMENT MESSAGE

A Biblical-Theological Commentary

Wilfrid Harrington, O.P. and Donald Senior, C.P.

EDITORS

New Testament Message, Volume 15

COLOSSIANS

Patrick V. Rogers, C.P.

Michael Glazier, Inc.
Wilmington, Delaware

MICHAEL GLAZIER, INC.
1210A King Street
Wilmington, Delaware 19801

Library of Congress Catalog Card Number: 80-83063
International Standard Book Number
    New Testament Message series: 0-89453-123-9
    COLOSSIANS: 0-89453-138-7

Printed in the United States of America by Abbey Press

Contents

ACKNOWLEDGMENTS

My sincere gratitude is due to Fr. Wilfrid Harrington who encouraged me to undertake this commentary, to my colleagues at Milltown Institute who made helpful suggestions while it was in progress, and to Mrs. Nora Davitt who so cheerfully typed the text from my almost illegible handwritten notes.

DEDICATION

This book is dedicated to my Passionist confreres in Ireland and Scotland.

Patrick Rogers

EDITORS' PREFACE

New Testament Message is a commentary series designed to bring the best of biblical scholarship to a wide audience. Anyone who is sensitive to the mood of the church today is aware of a deep craving for the Word of God. This interest in reading and praying the scriptures is not confined to a religious elite. The desire to strengthen one's faith and to mature in prayer has brought Christians of all types and all ages to discover the beauty of the biblical message. Our age has also been heir to an avalanche of biblical scholarship. Recent archaeological finds, new manuscript evidence, and the increasing volume of specialized studies on the Bible have made possible a much more profound penetration of the biblical message. But the flood of information and its technical nature keeps much of this scholarship out of the hands of the Christian who is eager to learn but is not a specialist. *New Testament Message* is a response to this need.

The subtitle of the series is significant: "A Biblical-Theological Commentary." Each volume in the series, while drawing on up-to-date scholarship, concentrates on bringing to the fore in understandable terms the specific message of each biblical author. The essay-format (rather than a word-by-word commentary) helps the reader savor the beauty and power of the biblical message and, at the same time, understand the sensitive task of responsible biblical interpretation.

A distinctive feature of the series is the amount of space given to the "neglected" New Testament writings, such as Colossians, James, Jude, the Pastoral Letters, the Letters of Peter and John. These briefer biblical books make a significant but often overlooked contribution to the richness of the New Testament. By assigning larger than normal coverage to these books, the series hopes to give these parts of Scripture the attention they deserve.

Because *New Testament Message* is aimed at the entire English speaking world, it is a collaborative effort of international proportions. The twenty-two contributors represent biblical scholarship in North America, Britain, Ireland and Australia. Each of the contributors is a recognized expert in his or her field, has published widely, and has been chosen because of a proven ability to communicate at a popular level. And, while all of the contributors are Roman Catholic, their work is addressed to the Christian community as a whole. The New Testament is the patrimony of all Christians.It is the hope of all concerned with this series that it will bring a fuller appreciation of God's saving Word to his people.

Wilfrid Harrington, O.P.
Donald Senior, C.P.

INTRODUCTION

MANY COMMENTARIES have appeared upon the letter of Paul to the Colossians, since that dynamic little document was first studied by the christian faithful, almost twenty centuries ago. In view of so many previous publications devoted to the problems and splendours of this epistle, one's first thought before embarking upon yet another must be: What further need have we of commentaries? Is there any particular value in examining yet again, without prospect or pretension to saying the last word upon the subject?

Paul's inspired epistles, being our first and most primitive heritage from the apostolic age, need continual reappraisal by each generation and by each individual believer, if they are to speak their message heart to heart. There is a proper sense in which "private interpretation" can be recommended, is indeed indispensable, since ultimately it is we ourselves who must discern what the Scriptures are saying to us, as we read them through the filter of our own personal history and preoccupations. But private understanding stands to benefit richly from knowing the responses, questions and enthusiasms of others, faced by the same inspired text. Within the ecclesial community of faith, indeed, we allow our understanding of God's Word to be guided by the commonly-held doctrine of the Church, yet we also need the stimulus of contemporary questions and fresh responses to bring us into vital contact with the mind of St. Paul.

In this commentary, I have aimed to present a personal reaction to his message, taking cognizance of (and sometimes quoting from) other commentaries, but all the while trying to capture the challenge which is implicit in St. Paul's words. If use is frequently made of the first-person plural, it is from the conviction that the epistle is addressed to us today just as surely as it once was to the Colossians. Like the Exodus saga, it was written "for our instruction, upon whom the final age has come" (1 Cor 10:11). I must confess that the close reading of this epistle can prove a rather difficult and even daunting project, condensing as it does some of the most profound and complex of the apostle's ideas. Yet such is the richness of its subject-matter that any labour undertaken to understand it will be more than amply repaid.

Understandably, the reading of letters written in antiquity is generally left to the scholarly taste of historians, antiquarians and literary critics. Not so with the letters of Paul, portions of which form a regular part of our public worship. They are so used in the belief that, by listening, we will be inspired and motivated towards conversion while being also instructed in matters of doctrine. Without any doubt, Paul has exercised enormous influence on christian faith and practise in ages past. His apostolic status and Christ-centred insight help to explain the huge volume of quotations from the epistles, in the writings of the theologians and Fathers of the Church.

Paul's life-story is already well known to the readers of this commentary. It reveals a many-sided character, whose viewpoint can often be complex but never boring. "He was an enthusiast and a mystic, with powers of rapt contemplation beyond the common. But he was also one who could apply the cold criticism of reason to his own dreams. This combination of enthusiasm with sanity is one of his eminent marks of greatness. His thought is strong and soaring, adventurous rather than systematic" (C.H. Dodd: *The Meaning of Paul for Today*, p.28). These traits of mystical enthusiasm and sober realism are quite discernible in the epistle to the Colossians, giving it that zest which cannot but be relevant to anybody interested in living Christianity.

Today also, the letters of this apostle hold their place among the writings through which God speaks to men, "enlightening their minds, strengthening their wills and setting their hearts on fire with love" (Vatican II, *Dei Verbum*, par. 21). Through good and readable translations, the rushing current of his thought remains accessible to the many believers who are willing to submit themselves to the Pauline experience. But in order to appreciate the richness of this vision and thus get a maximum of benefit from individual passages, we need to understand the background, aims and structure of the individual epistles. This must be briefly attempted for Colossians, before proceeding to a more detailed comment upon the text itself. Once the peculiarities and special concerns of this epistle are grasped in broad outline, it becomes easier to let the heart beat in unison with the throbbing intensity which is here displayed by the great-hearted apostle of the gentiles. To the attentive reader, his words to Colossae can live again and be for us what they have been for so many others – words of life.

Destination Colossae

Colossae was a small city in Phrygia, in the southwestern section of modern Turkey. Set on the bank of the Lycus river, whose narrow valley provided the main East-West route from the Aegean coast through the Phrygian mountains, Colossae was well-known to the historians of antiquity. It is mentioned as a "great city" in the fifth century B.C., when the Persians under Xerxes passed through it, on their way to invade Greece. Xenophon described it as "prosperous and large," in the year 401 B.C., as he passed through with the retreating army of Cyrus the younger. This age of splendour had waned somewhat, in the days of St. Paul. Colossae was overshadowed in size and prosperity by two more recently founded towns: Hierapolis and Laodicea, both within a radius of twelve miles and both receiving mention in our epistle (Col 4:13-15).

The whole region, well known in those days for its woolen industry (Strabo praises the fine black wool of the local sheep), belonged to the Roman province of Asia which was governed from Ephesus, some sixty miles to the north-west. It was devastated by earthquake towards the end of the first century, and Colossae simply disappeared, never to be rebuilt. Only in the nineteenth century was the site identified again, when excavation revealed portions of a theatre and an acropolis, but little else. So we must content ourselves with less knowledge of Colossae than with the destinations of the other epistles of St. Paul.

It is clear from Col 1:7 and 2:1 that Paul is without direct, first-hand knowledge of the Christian community in Colossae, although he is deeply concerned for their welfare and prays for their progress in faith. The church there must, however, have been founded under the influence of the apostle during the third of his great missionary journeys. Very probably this was done through Epaphras, himself from Colossae and a valued colleague of Paul's (1:7), during the apostle's quite lengthy stay in Ephesus (Acts 19). Although Paul must have passed quite close to Colossae at the beginning of his third journey, as he "went from place to place through Galatia and Phrygia" (Acts 18:23), it remained one of the few towns not visited by him. During the next two years he used Ephesus as his base of activities and performed a thorough evangelization of that region, with the help of friends like Timothy, Tychicus and Epaphras. Allowing for some outraged exaggeration on the part of Demetrius the silversmith, it seems quite sure that "almost throughout all Asia, this Paul has persuaded a considerable number of people" (Acts 19:26). Accordingly, we should regard the Colossian Christians as a Pauline church, imbued with the same spirit and doctrine as those at Thessalonika, Philippi, Corinth and Ephesus.

Was it a large community, and how was it composed? Apart from a few hints within the epistle itself, we cannot tell. The personal references in 4:7-17 suggest a small, closely-knit group, all known to each other by name. Yet it also appears that they included a good cross-section both of age and status, parents and children, masters and slaves (3:18-4:1) and possibly also a racial background (3:11). That it was open to other currents of religious thought is obvious from the polemical section (2:8-23). It was this danger of heterodoxy indeed which caused our epistle to be written in the first place. Leader of the community was apparently Archippus (4:17), who presumably succeeded Epaphras when the latter went to stay with Paul at Ephesus. It is reasonable therefore to imagine the church at Colossae as consisting of a few dozen people, united in faith and friendship, coming together regularly in somebody's house (4:15) for prayer, instruction and the Eucharist, under the pastoral care of a man who had received his ministry "in the Lord" by a kind of rudimentary apostolic succession.

A significant detail to note is the contact he maintained between the faithful at Colossae and those at Laodicea (and Hierapolis). Letters from Paul to one community were to be passed on to others (4:16), thereby fostering their awareness of belonging to a Church that was much broader than its local manifestation, was indeed world-wide, and had as its head none other than Christ himself.

Why it was written

Several motives no doubt combined to urge Paul to write to Colossae, among them his genuine friendly feeling towards the good Christians living there, and the desire to establish a direct relationship in order to share with them his special gifts of encouragement and doctrine. But the immediate occasion for the letter was his fear that a dangerous error would gain ground among the Colossians, and ruin their faith in Christ. We may assume that it was from his friend Epaphras that Paul learned of this heretical tendency, as well as of the fundamental faith and goodwill of the community. Our knowledge of this heresy is therefore only third-hand, through Paul's reaction to another's report. If we find it difficult to combine his various disparaging references into one coherent heresy, this would lead us to think of several rival schols of thought at Colossae rather than a united front of unorthodoxy.

The tendencies against which Paul warns are these:

1. *Pseudo-philosophy:* The warning against "philosophy and vain deceit" (2:8) suggests that some were opposing or diluting the Gospel message in the name of another brand of wisdom, a merely human shrewdness which is opposed to the wisdom of God (cf. 1 Cor 2:6). Their viewpoint was doubtless an earlier version of that Gnosticism which posed such a major threat to the Church in the second century. No doubt, Paul's use of some popular philosophic terms ("fulness" 1:19; "knowledge" 2:3; "severity to the body" 2:23) is prompted by some aberrations connected with these terms among the Colossians.

2. *False Asceticism:* The proper ethical liberty of the faithful to choose and to use all the good gifts of God the creator was being threatened by some who warned "do not handle, do not taste, do not touch" (2:21). This ascetic group regarded certain kinds of food and drink as decadent or morally harmful, and purported to pass judgment upon others who might not abide by their prohibitions (2:16). We can discern a particularly Jewish flavour in this rigorism, especially in the reference to "festivals, new moons and sabbath" (2:16). When in this context we also find explicit mention of "circumcision," now reinterpreted to mean a spiritual rebirth (2:11-13), there can be no doubt

that a Judaizing influence was the root cause of at least a part of the Colossian problem.

3. *Worship of Angels:* Some pressure was being brought to bear upon the Colossians to combine their worship of Christ with a reverential abasement towards other intermediaries of divinity, the "elemental spirits of the universe" (2:8). Paul rejects this pressure (2:18), by insisting that Christians have died with Christ to these elemental spirits (2:20), and need no longer submit to their regulation. Where did this angel-worship arise? Not from biblical Judaism, certainly, with its vigorous and thoroughgoing monotheism. If Paul's warning is against the Gentile tenets from which the Colossians were converted, its reference would be to some segment of the pagan pantheon. On the other hand, a mingling of strange mythology with the traditional Old Testament faith is known to have held sway in some Jewish nonconformist circles, which were themselves influenced by surrounding pagan notions. If we are to think of the Colossian problem as arising from a single group, it would have to be one which syncretized Judaism with alien elements in this way. Many commentators are attracted by Lightfoot's view that the best analogy for the Colossian heresy is found in the Essene sect, combining mystical speculation, ascetical practises and a strong interest in – perhaps even worship of – angels.

Whether or not these tendencies already existed in a unitary system elsewhere, it is not surprising that an amalgam of them should accumulate within such a bustling cosmopolitan area as the Lycus valley, with its considerable Jewish population and keen awareness of the multiple cult-forms to the heathen gods. The atmosphere at Colossae was as open to syncretism as is that of the liberal Western world today and thus militated against a centralizing of faith, confidence and service in the one mediator, Jesus Christ.

The seriousness of the error at Colossae lay in drawing people away from the true source of salvation (Christ) and into the "shadow" as opposed to the substance (2:17). The obvious danger of attempting to combine christian faith with submission to directives coming from elsewhere (through "visions" and the "sensuous mind" 2:18), would be "not holding fast to the Head" (2:19), nothing less than self-inflicted excommunication. It is worth noting how the Apostle meets this danger with argument and vibrant exhortation, rather than by denunciation of persons. His appeal is to religious experience and to faith, rather than to formal authority. In a curious way, too, we have reason to be grateful for the stimulus caused by the Colossian heresy, which "would have disappeared without leaving any trace in the annals of human thought, if it had not provoked Paul into writing his fullest statement of the universal sovereignty of Christ" (G.B. Caird).

Composed by St. Paul

In the opening verse of the epistle, the author claims to be Paul the apostle – and Colossians has been included in the list of Paul's writings as far back as we can trace. The external evidence for its authenticity is therefore very strong. However, since the mid-nineteenth century a small minority of critics has challenged this evidence, on grounds internal to the epistle itself. Reasons adduced against ascribing Colossians to Paul can be grouped under three headings: Language, Style and Doctrine, in all of which it differs so much from the earlier epistles that (the critics maintain) it cannot come from the same author.

The *language* of Colossians is remarkable for a number of words and phrases not found in the major epistles. These include "inheritance" (1:12) "making peace" (1:20), "complete what is lacking" (1:24), "dwells bodily" (2:9); along with a series of expressions specifically employed against the adversaries at Colossae: "beguiling speech," "make a prey," "new moon," "worship of angels," and "severity to the body." On the other hand, it is impossible to limit

Paul's vocabulary to the range of words used in Romans, Corinthians, Thessalonians and whatever other epistles one might denote as unassailably genuine. Each of the epistles contains its own special characteristics of vocabulary, much of it dictated by the actual circumstances to which it was addressed. One must also allow for some development of theological vocabulary by Paul himself in the course of his ministry, during which he undoubtedly discussed the christian faith with others who enriched his thought, even as he enriched theirs.

In its *style* also, Colossians appears to exhibit some peculiarities laden with participles and subordinate clauses, resulting in several very lengthy and untidy sentences, such as 1:3-6 and 1:9-12 and 1:24-27. Paul's earlier style was usually more rapid and lucid, although this was not always so. There are passages like 2 Cor 9:12-14 that are just as long and convoluted as the sentence-structure in Colossians, indicating that one cannot seriously challenge Pauline authorship on the basis of style alone.

The *doctrinal content* of Colossians has some striking parallels to the thought of earlier epistles, but also a few notable shifts of emphasis. Its christology, as we shall see, is highly developed upon a cosmic scale, with Jesus portrayed as the one through whom all things were created, and in whom they hold together. Would the earlier Paul have spoken of Christ as "Head" of the "Body" (the Church), and not rather as himself the Body into whom all the baptized are incorporated? Still, one may not force the apostle's thought into a uniformly consistent set of metaphors, nor prevent him from extending the range of an image which he has used differently elsewhere. Thus he can move from regarding the cross as simply the means of mankind's redemption (Rom 5:6-11) to making it the source of universal reconciliation for all things, whether on earth or in heaven (Col 1:20).

On the other hand, Colossians does contain strong features of the apostle's distinctive style. How typical of him to begin with praise and encouragement before offering any word of rebuke or advice; to cite his own living experience as an example of God's working within the Church; to be vigorous in rejecting what he perceives as a threat to Christian freedom; and to centre his message upon the powerful cross of Christ. His mystic communion with Christ's Passion links this epistle with 2 Cor 4:10, Gal 2:20 and Phil 3:10. Many other similarities will be mentioned in the course of our commentary, indicating the consistency of Colossians within the whole range of Paul's thought. Whatever is special in our epistle can be attributed partly to the provocation of the dangerous trends at Colossae and partly to the sheer mental vitality of the apostle, whose abundant repertoire of ideas provided a response tailor-made to the needs of each community. Nor may we ignore the progression of Paul's own understanding, as he achieved further insights into his ongoing life-experience. One who prayed so fervently for the development of spiritual understanding among his readers (1:9) can hardly have shut himself off from a similar interior growth.

Paul pays his readers the compliment of presuming in them a high level of doctrinal understanding and of moral idealism. His epistle packs into four short chapters a resume of the most fundamental christian themes, requiring a slow and reflective assimilation on our part. In its density, Colossians represents the distilled essence of thoughts which are elsewhere expounded at greater length. It has been remarked that no other writing of St. Paul is "more vigorous in concept or more instinct with meaning. If there is a want of fluency, there is no lack of force" (Lightfoot). This Pauline combination of power and brevity will, I hope, justify what might otherwise appear to be excessively long comments upon individual words or verses.

The Place and Time of Composition

The apostle could have spared his commentators a considerable labour of deduction had he chosen to mention the precise circumstances in which each of his letters was written. Since he did not do so, clues must be sought within the texts themselves. These must first be compared with scraps of significant information within his other epistles and then built into a single hypothesis which dovetails plausibly with the general outline of his ministry given in Acts. He does state that Colossians was written from prison (1:24; 4:10), but when and where? The best answer we can hope for is a well-informed guess. The jail-periods at Caesarea (Acts 23:33ff) and Rome Acts 28:16ff) are the most obvious candidates. However, there is good reason to think that he was also imprisoned for a time at Ephesus (cf. 1 Cor 15:32; 2 Cor 1:8; 11:23), and Clement of Rome states that Paul was in prison seven times (letter to Corinth 5:6).

A significant clue to the most likely origin of Colossians is its close association with the short letter to Philemon. Since both texts mention the same people – Timothy, Aristarchus, Mark, Epaphras, Luke, Demas and One-simus, the runaway slave about whose future Paul wrote to Philemon – it seems very likely that both were written at about the same time, and from the same imprisonment. In which case, Caesarea should be ruled out as a possible place of origin, as it is most unlikely that Paul's contact with Onesimus occurred during his two-year military arrest there (Acts 24:27, A.D. 58-60), under the procurator Felix.

A better case might be made for situating both Phm and Col during Paul's supposed prison-period at Ephesus not mentioned in Acts, sometime between A.D. 54-57. This theory would fit the apostle's expectation of an early release, after which he will visit Philemon (Phm 22) at nearby Colossae. Such proximity might also serve to explain Paul's interest in a local christian community which had not been directly founded by himself. On the other hand, it is hardly likely that the runaway slave (Onesimus) would try to hide within so short a distance of his master's wrath. Would he not have headed to Rome, because it was distant and cosmopolitan rather than for Ephesus, barely a hundred miles from home. If we think of Colossians and

Philemon as both written from Rome – which is the more widely-held view – then it appears that Paul envisaged another journey to the East, after his release from prison. Such a late date for Colossians during the Roman captivity of A.D. 61-63 (Acts 28:30) would give a satisfactory background to its highly-developed doctrine of Christ and the church. Then, as to the practical motive urging Paul to concern himself so much with a tiny community, hundreds of miles away, which he had not yet visited, this can be quite adequately explained by his friendship with Onesimus and with others from Colossae whom he had met elsewhere.

On balance, then, we opt for Rome as the most likely location, and for A.D. 61 (with recent hardships fresh in memory, Col 1:24) as the probable date of our epistle.

Central Theme: Christ's Person and Work

St. Paul's response to the errors threatening at Colossae was to give a fuller and richer description of Jesus Christ as man's Saviour. Although the person of Christ constitutes the unifying centre of all the New Testament writings, seldom is he described in such exalted and profound terms as by this epistle. In texts that will be fully considered at their proper place, Paul portrays Christ as the Son and Image of God, first-born of all creation, head of the church, pre-eminent in all things. He is the one in whom dwells the fullness of God, and through whom all things are reconciled with the Father. His word dwells within those who believe, and through him they grow to spiritual maturity, living by a renewed life because they have died in him, and now his peace rules their hearts. Phrase piles upon phrase, as Paul strives for a fuller description of the Lord. He is the Mystery of God, the Treasury of all wisdom and knowledge, the very Hope of glory. During even a rapid reading of the epistle, expressions conveying a glorious vision of Christ leap to the eye. If we accept that they were written within about thirty years of the Master's crucifixion (as we have maintained), these words to Colossae constitute the remarkable summit of the whole of Pauline christology.

We might well be amazed to find such exalted phrases being affirmed of a man who had publicly died by ignominious death within the span of living memory. Where did Paul get his vision of Christ, or find the language to express it as he does? To this question we can propose at least a tentative and partial answer. The great Apostle could speak in this way, and even desire to complete in his own flesh what was lacking in Our Lord's sufferings (1:24) on account of a powerful direct experience of the risen Christ. This experience, which already made its impact on the earlier epistles (1 Th 1:10; 4:14; 1 Cor 15:3-8; 2 Cor 3:17-21; Gal 2:20; 5:1; Rom 1:4-6; Phil 3:7-11, etc.) formed the solid basis for Paul's Christ-centred proclamation of faith. On the other hand, this preaching would hardly have been possible, and certainly would not have been effective, unless the glory of the risen Lord also found its reflection in the hearts of the hearers. Their gift of faith was proportionate to the mighty conviction of the Apostle. Even if they sometimes required admonition to preserve them from relapse into unbelief, their general grasp of the apostolic message was such that a sublime doctrine of Christ could effectively be preached to them – and through them to us.

OUTLINE OF THE EPISTLE TO THE COLOSSIANS

I. TRUE PASTORAL INTEREST [1:1-14]

Opening greeting (1-2)
Thanksgiving for their progress thus far (3-8)
Prayer for further growth in the spirit (9-14)

II. DOCTRINAL SECTION: The identity and role of Christ [1:15 – 2:23]

The great Christology (15-20)
Reconciliation and firmness (21-23)
Apostolic mediation through suffering (1:24-29)
A special kind of encouragement (2:1-7)
Our cancelled bondage (8-15)
The wrong recipe (16-19)
True and false submission (20-23)

III. MORAL SECTION: Living the Risen Life [3:1 – 4:6]

Foundations (3:1-4)
The old way and the new (3:5-10)
Mankind reunited (3:11)
Vestments of harmony (3:12-14)
The fullness of peace (3:15-17)
Home and family life (3:18 – 4:1)
Prayer, zeal and prudence (4:2-6)

IV. WORDS OF ENCOURAGEMENT AND FAREWELL [4:7-18]

The bearers of the letter (7-9)
Greetings from several people (10-14)
Messages to several others (15-17)
Farewell Signature (18)

COMMENTARY

I. True Pastoral Interest (1:1-14)

AN APOSTOLIC GREETING.
1:1-2.

> **1** Paul, an apostle of Christ Jesus by the will of God, and Timothy our brother, [2]To the saints and faithful brethren in Christ at Colossae: Grace to you and peace from God our Father.

PAUL INTRODUCES HIMSELF in his usual way, by name and by vocation, establishing between himself and his readers a relationship which is both personal and official. In earlier letters it was his practise to elaborate further on the circumstances of his vocation, whereby he was "set apart for the gospel of God" (Rom 1:1) by an exceptional conversion "after the due season" (1 Cor 15:8). Now writing towards the end of his career, it is enough to identify himself as an apostle of Christ Jesus, since at this stage he was well known and acknowledged among the churches of Asia Minor and Greece.

His preaching mission was not a merely private initiative, but a service demanded by the will of God. This idea features clearly in the introduction to several of Paul's letters

(1 Cor, 2 Cor, Eph), without any obvious motive for polemical self-defence. There was no need to prove his apostolic status to the Colossians as though it had been doubted by them or impugned as in Galatia (Gal 1-2); yet it comes spontaneously to mention the divine impetus underlying his mission. What never ceased to excite his wonder was the manner whereby God chose the most unlikely instruments for the spread of the Gospel. His own selection as apostle seemed a living proof of divine mercy towards those who had gone astray (cf. 1 Tim 1:16). Hence we find in no other New Testament writer such a profound awareness of the gift of vocation.

Ever courteous, he places the name of Timothy alongside his own in this opening greeting. Acknowledgement of interdependence with others is surely among the most gracious of leadership qualities, and one which encourages the continuing cooperation of one's helpers. Paul counted Timothy, who was perhaps twenty years his junior, among his closest assistants ever since their first encounter many years previously (Acts 16:1; 1 Tim 4:12; 2 Tim 1:5). Other texts combine to show how this friendship lasted throughout the apostle's travels (Acts 19:22; 20:4; 1 Th 1:1; 2 Cor 1:1; Rom 16:21) and right up to his final imprisonment (2 Tim 4:9-13). The relationship suggested here is that between fraternal colleagues jointly engaged in the work of evangelization (compare the more paternal tone of the Pastoral Epistles). Still, this joint salutation should not be interpreted as declaring complete apostolic equality between Paul and Timothy. Paul's unique sense of his own mission was in no way diminished by his cordial association of others with himself as fellow-workers in the Lord's vineyard; always he remained the special "ambassador" to the Gentiles (2 Cor 5:20; Gal 2:8; cf. 2 Cor 11:23).

Addressed as "saints" and "faithful," the Colossian Christians receive two of Paul's highest epithets of praise acknowledging their status as a consecrated people. Elsewhere his greetings are often directed to the local church as such ("to the church of God at Corinth," "to the church of the Thessalonians"), but here he prefers the more personal, distributive phrase which each individual reader may take as directed to himself or herself. As well as being complimentary, "saints" and "faithful" also contain the implicit challenge to live in a way worthy of God's special elect – a point which is spelled out in the ethical half of the epistle, from 3:1 onward. For the present it is enough to notice a minor difference of emphasis between "saints" (being set apart from the sinful world to share in the holiness of God) and "faithful" (actually living in accordance with that high vocation). Do these words contain some hint that not all the Christians at Colossae have remained loyal, so that Paul would be greeting only an elite wing of the church? This seems unlikely, despite the warnings in the following chapter against those who were leading others astray. The greeting is not meant to divide the community into loyal and renegade; its focus upon fidelity "does not directly exclude any, but indirectly warns all" (Lightfoot). All of its readers had experienced the call to holiness, and would understand that they still stood within its uplifting influence.

What the early Christians wished each other was not simply "health, happiness and prosperity" but "grace and peace," acknowledging that only by God's gift can man have deep and lasting joy. "Peace," that "Shalom" which the Old Testament prophets longed to see, entailed all the blessings of the Messianic age, especially reconciliation and union with God. Its use as a greeting derives from Christ himself (Mt 10:12; Mk 5:34; Lk 24:36) and is typical of the New Testament epistles, from which it flows into our liturgy. Quite unusual, however, is the invocation of the Father's name alone, without mention of Jesus Christ as the co-author of grace and peace. The same concentration

upon the Father will be found in the next verse, for a definite
purpose within the context of this epistle.

THANKSGIVING FOR THEIR PROGRESS
THUS FAR.
1:3-8.

The pastoral strategy evident in Paul's life and writings
is based upon the encouraging belief that just as divine
grace has already touched the lives of his converts so it
will continue to upbuild them to their full spiritual statures.
Accordingly, he begins with words of appreciation, helping
the readers recognize their dignity as people endowed with
the seed of divine life (1 Th 1:2-10; 2 Th 1:3-4; 1 Cor 1:4-9
etc). Precisely this relationship of pastoral respect provides
the most fruitful basis for the challenging moral ideals to
follow. Furthermore, his expectations are often couched
in the form of prayer rather than of authoritative demand;
and though anxious about dangers in the immediate present
his predominant attitude is optimistic both as regards what
has already begun among the faithful and what remains
to be achieved.

> [3]We always thank God, the Father of our Lord Jesus
> Christ, when we pray for you, [4]because we have heard
> of your faith in Christ Jesus and of the love which you
> have for all the saints, [5]because of the hope laid up for you
> in heaven. Of this you have heard before in the word of
> the truth, the gospel [6]which has come to you, as indeed in
> the whole world it is bearing fruit and growing—so
> among yourselves, from the day you heard and under-
> stood the grace of God in truth, [7]as you learned it from
> Epaphras our beloved fellow servant. He is a faithful
> minister of Christ on our behalf [8]and has made known to
> us your love in the Spirit.

These hallmarks of St. Paul's pastoral style – thanksgiving and prayer – occur very early in this Epistle. His

untiring christian concern for others flows readily into prayer on their behalf, remembering them with love in the presence of God and asking for their good. His special petitions on behalf of this particular community will be specified later in terms of moral growth and development (vv.9-11). But before pointing out their need for fuller spiritual maturity he first gives thanks for the good fruits of virtue borne by them and praises their faith and their love. Every prayer of his for others has this lovely background of appreciation of that grace of God which is already at work and fruitful.

In the large majority of cases, early christian prayer is explicitly directed towards the Eternal Father through the Son, on the conviction that God is our father precisely because he is first the father of Jesus Christ, into whom we are incorporated. However, there is good reason for the special focus here upon the primacy of the Father. In the remainder of this epistle, attention will be centred mainly upon the role of Jesus as man's Saviour; but this is done within the clear understanding of referring all things ultimately to God the Father.

Somebody, presumably Epaphras, has reported favourably to Paul about the state of spirituality among the Colossians. Accordingly they are praised for manifesting the three essential interlocking qualities of faith, love and hope. First, they had faith in Christ Jesus, believing in him as their living Lord and therefore committed to him in faithful service. For Paul, faith was never merely doctrinal assent but always included this pragmatic dimension of fidelity. Faith led necessarily to love for all those other believers who also shared the life of Christ. The precise relationship of their faith and love to hope is a little puzzling here. Normally one would think that hope springs from faith, but now the order has been inverted, so that the faith and love of the Colossians appear to depend upon a future hope laid up in the heavens. The most straightforward meaning is that their strong trust in the blessed future which God has in store for them formed the basis for their fidelity and love here in this present life. This might sound a somewhat mercenary motive for christian living until we remember how much their hope was centred upon the person of the risen Christ himself. Hope contains both a present and a future dimension: already they had a personal taste of Christ through faith and community sharing, but they looked forward to a fuller possession of his love and friendship in the age to come.

The gospel, as preached to the Colossians and accepted by them, is not only *good* (in the sense of being a hopeful message and a powerful stimulus to moral growth) but also *true*. This insistence upon the truth of the gospel prepares us for Paul's attack upon false doctrines which were competing for the allegiance of his readers. They must value the genuine gospel as they first heard it from Epaphras, and not be taken in by any spurious substitute for it (cf. Gal 1:6).

Paul now makes a strong personification of the gospel message as the living extension of Christ, who through it brings spiritual growth to the hearers (v.6). The same gospel which has been fruitful in other places has proved its power also at Colossae. Universality confirms both its truth and its power. "The false gospels are the outgrowths of local circumstances: the true gospel is the same everywhere" (Lightfoot). The fruitfulness of the Word is described in a botanical image deriving from Jesus's own parables of the Sower (Mk 4:3-8) or the Vine and the Branches (Jn 15:1-8). There is something slightly odd about the sequence "bearing fruit and growing," when the normal process would be first growth, then fruit. This peculiarity should hardly be forced to yield such an explicit sense as: "the gospel is not like those plants that exhaust themselves in bearing fruit and then wither away; its external growth keeps pace with its reproductive energy" (Lightfoot). More sober is John Chrysostom's explanation that the gospel first bore fruit through deeds and then grew by being accepted by many people. This would make complete sense of the image, if we understand the "fruit" to refer to the immediate effect of the gospel message upon the lives of the first believers and the "growth" as the consequent conversion of others impressed by this example.

The Colossians had themselves played an honourable part in the growth of the gospel, because of their prompt acceptance of it. They appreciated its value from the beginning and recognized it as God's loving plan for their salvation. Their cooperation with the gospel of grace (cf. Acts 20:24) was such that Paul could hold them up as an example to other christian communities just as he had earlier done with the Thessalonians (1 Th 1:7).

Ever willing to give credit where it was due, Paul acknowledges the vital contribution of his friend and colleague Epaphras, who had planted the gospel at Colossae. This man gets the honourable designation *fellow-servant*, just as the apostle so often refers to himself as the servant of God, of Christ, or of the Gospel. Epaphras had in fact performed a double service. As well as preaching the gospel to the community at Colossae, he reported back from them to Paul, so helping to forge a link between the apostle and that local church. As we have seen already he was able to bring a positive report: genuine christian charity (*agapē*) was alive at Colossae. Their love for one another was *in the Spirit* or under the impulse of the Holy Spirit (cf. Gal 5:22; Rom 14:17) and no mere passing affection under the fickle sway of one's benevolent mood.

PRAYER FOR FURTHER GROWTH IN THE SPIRIT. 1:9-14.

> [9]And so, from the day we heard of it, we have not ceased to pray for you, asking that you may be filled with the knowledge of his will in all spiritual wisdom and understanding, [10]to lead a life worthy of the Lord, fully pleasing to him, bearing fruit in every good work and increasing in the knowledge of God. [11]May you be strengthened with all power, according to his glorious

> might, for all endurance and patience with joy, [12]giving
> thanks to the Father, who has qualified us to share in the
> inheritance of the saints in light. [13]He has delivered us
> from the dominion of darkness and transferred us to the
> kingdom of his beloved Son, [14]in whom we have re-
> demption, the forgiveness of sins.

Whatever initial achievement of faith and love was
evident amongst the community, there was still a need for
fuller growth, both in understanding and behaviour. It was
the sound practice of the apostle first to praise and then to
appeal to further effort, thus presenting the christian life
as a continual process of growth towards full maturity in
Christ. Here he puts his appeal in the form of a prayer,
furnishing us with a magnificent model of how to approach
God and what to request from him. We should bring our
prayers to God without ceasing, and the burden of our
petitions must be a) for the discernment of his will, and
b) for the power to fulfil that will in our lives.

Whoever desires a more godly way of life must first pray
for an increase of wisdom. It was a long-established maxim
of the Greek philosophers that virtue and knowledge go
hand in hand and reinforce each other. Paul, who had little
regard for Greek philosophic speculation as such, had to
specify the particular kind of wisdom or understanding
which would support christian life. What he prays for is
spiritual understanding, something far removed from the
short-sighted argumentative opinions upon which people so
often pride themselves. Christian wisdom begins with
humble, admiring awareness of the will of God. It recognizes that his will is identical with love and sees moral duty
as man's loving response to the call of prior, divine love.
Each of the Pauline captivity letters shows concern for this
brand of wisdom (Phil 1:9; Eph 1:17; Philem 6). His concern at
this point for the contemplative aspect of the gospel can be
explained "partly by his personal circumstances, partly by
the requirements of the Church"(Lightfoot). Imprisonment

with its enforced leisure would lead Paul's personal thoughts in that direction, while outside his prison the danger threatening the Church from heretical speculation also required new emphasis upon the wisdom of the gospel.

Fruit and proof of christian wisdom will be the high standard of godly behaviour described in the following three verses. Such achievement is possible not by our own efforts but by the power of divine grace and so this section upon behaviour worthy of our God will flow easily into a hymn to our Redeemer.

Christian living is described both in terms of activity and of patience. Actively they must strive, as Israel in the past had so often failed to do, to walk worthily of the Lord (1 Th 2:12; Eph 4:1), a people conducting their lives in the spirit of pilgrimage, walking in the ways of the Lord. The word *pleasing* applies to the attitude of genuine worship, in contrast to the unworthy subservience often shown towards human rulers (1 Th 2:4; Gal 1:10). To gain God's approval remains always for Paul the highest aim and object of life (Rom 12:1-2; 14:18; 1 Cor 7:32). It prepares the way for a variety of good works which in turn open our minds to a fuller understanding of the will of God. There is a most fruitful interplay here between knowing and doing the will of God.

Though highly compressed, the meaning of verse 11 is fairly straightforward. It acknowledges the need for courage in the life of faith, and shows the source of that courage. In order to stand fast in the face of difficulties whether from outside or from within ourselves, we need a power of endurance. This is no mere stoical patience to be achieved by deliberate, ruthless extinction of our feelings, but rather a hopeful perseverance which is elevated by joy and whose motivation is from above. The glorious light of God, a phrase that evokes the memory of the resurrection of Jesus from the dead (Rom 6:4) is the dynamic which guides the whole course of creation and in particular the destiny of man. This conviction is part of our heritage from Israel, as is the luminous symbol of "glory" for the outward manifestation of the divine power and the sign of his presence among his people. Just as during the ministry of Jesus power flowed out from him to heal those who were in need, so now in his risen glory he is the channel of God's power for all who trust in him.

Is there some slight distinction between endurance and patience? Both of them refer to a quality of maturity able to cope with a hostile environment. Endurance is a habit of mind which resists any rapid collapse into despondence in the face of suffering, while patience is a self restraint which does not hastily retaliate against a wrong committed by another. One author has neatly explained endurance as "refusal to be daunted by hard times" and patience as "refusal to be upset by perverse people" (Caird). It is characteristic of Paul to insist that despite hardship and suffering the gift of joy will continue to be given (Gal 5:22; Phil 1:18), a joy so firmly rooted in faith and trust that no setback or suffering can quite dislodge it from the heart. "It is easy to be joyful when things go well, but the christian radiance is something which not all the shadows of life can quench" (Barclay).

Giving thanks to the Father: The basis for the unshakable joy of the faith occurs in the following three verses (12-14) which are a magnificent expression of christian gratitude for the gift of salvation. This beautiful spirit of thanksgiving pervades the whole epistle indeed (1:3; 2:7; 3:16-17; 4:2), but here at this point its basic motivation is most clearly explained. The growth in christian maturity which he prays for his readers will come to full flowering when they share his deep spirit of thankfulness.

The one to whom gratitude is due is God the Father, from whose gracious will comes the plan of our salvation. His loving graciousness is conveyed by the simple title, Father (Rom 6:4; 8:15; Eph 2:18; 3:14), whose saving will for us is made operative through his beloved Son. The place of the

Holy Spirit in our deliverance, though it is a profound conviction of Paul (Rom 8; Gal 5:16-25), receives only one fleeting mention in our epistle (1:8). Even so, he still presents salvation as a gift already received rather than as a prize to be won through striving. It is God who gives his people the competence and the ability to enter into the joy which he has planned for us.

Our "share in the inheritance of the saints in light" is a graphic phrase which might at first appear like a promise of heavenly glory in the world to come. Its immediate reference, however, is to what already belongs to the christian community here and now, namely our share in being (what Israel already was) the elect and the holy nation set apart as the Lord's own. The imagery is from the saga of the mosaic era and the conquest of the Promised Land, that special inheritance of God's holy people. That favour which Israel enjoyed in Yahweh's presence, metaphorically described as light or glory, is precisely what the christian people now enjoy through faith. It becomes still clearer in the following verses (13-14) that this inheritance is primarily the gift already granted rather than something to be hoped for in the future. The realm of light was a beloved image in the early church to describe the state of grace in which they found themselves, through Jesus the Light of the world (Jn 8:12). They were themselves to be light to others (Mt 5:14), or children of the light (1 Th 5:4), whose calling it was to walk in the light (Eph 5:8). "Light" therefore becomes a synonym for the kingdom of Christ, both in the present and in the future life.

Our "deliverance from the dominion of darkness" (v.13) continues the imagery of Exodus. The same mighty hand and outstretched arm of God which drew his people from Egyptian slavery had drawn the gentile Christians out from the darkness of pagan ways, ruled by sin. The expression "dominion of darkness" occurs in Lk 22:53, where the powers of evil hostile to Jesus seem on the verge of overwhelming him. The idea that conversion and faith transfer a person from one dominion to another is deep-rooted in the New Testament. In his defence before Agrippa, Paul describes his own mission to the Gentiles as having this junction: to open their eyes that they may *turn* from darkness to light and from the power of Satan to God (Acts 26:18). Similarly we are assured that God has called us out of darkness into his own wonderful light (1 Pet 2:9). The joy which pervades all these writings is based on the conviction that this transfer has already taken place and will remain permanent if only Christians stay faithful to their side of the covenant.

Our "transfer to the Kingdom of his Beloved Son" completes the Exodus image. The word transfer, which today evokes merely the change of a player from one football team to another, would have meant to Paul and his readers nothing less than the wholesale transportation of peoples to a new dwelling place, and specifically the passage of Israel through the desert to the promised land. Through their baptism, Christians have been carried over from the barren kingdom of Satan into the liberating kingdom of Jesus Christ. To come under the influence of Christ is to share in what he is, the child of God's love, the one in whom the Father is well pleased (Lk 3:22). It is most unusual to find the kingdom attributed to Christ rather than to God. However, this nuance fits quite appropriately within an epistle focussed upon the central role of Christ in our salvation. To him belongs the first stage of salvific leadership. He must rule until all enemies are subdued to him, and then hand over the kingdom to the Eternal Father, when the salvation of the universe will be complete (cf. 1 Cor 15:24-28).

After all that has preceded, it seems rather an anticlimax to equate redemption simply with forgiveness (v.14). Surely Paul does not wish to reduce the joy, the light, the heritage and the kingdom to the negative concept of ransom from sin! But he may well have included this phrase precisely to rule out some false concepts of what redemption meant. Mention of the forgiveness of sins illustrates very clearly how moral and spiritual is the conception of the kingdom of God in the New Testament. Redemption was neither political, in the sense willed by Jewish nationalistic zealots, nor any illusory, magical escape into immortality such as had been suggested by the heretical teachers at Colossae. Rather it was being saved from a sinful past at enmity with God and brought into his friendship, which required continual renunciation of those sins. Negative though it may sound, the forgiveness of sins here points towards its positive correlative: reconciliation with God, a theme which is taken up again immediately after the glorious hymn to Christ the Redeemer.

II. Doctrinal Section

THE GREAT CHRISTOLOGY.
1:15-20.

> [15]He is the image of the invisible God, the first-born of all creation; [16]for in him all things were created, in heaven and on earth, visible and invisible, whether thrones or dominions or principalities or authorities— all things were created through him and for him. [17]He is before all things, and in him all things hold together. [18]He is the head of the body, the church; he is the beginning, the first-born from the dead, that in everything he might be pre-eminent. [19]For in him all the fulness of God was pleased to dwell, [20]and through him to reconcile to himself all things, whether on earth or in heaven, making peace by the blood of his cross.

THIS SOARING HYMN which was prompted by the mention of redemption and launched from the high plateau of thanksgiving, carries us to the very pinnacle of Pauline christology. Its range and sweep are as vast as that other great hymn, the Johannine Prologue (Jn 1:1-18), its nearest New Testament equivalent. Both strive to give expression to the intimate bond between Christ and God, not only in the redemption of fallen humanity but in the very creation of the world. In the words of the fourth evangelist, Christ is identified as Word of God, who from the beginning was with God. For Paul he is the Image of the invisible God, in whom the divine fullness dwells. The apostle and the evangelist agree in revering him as the one mediator through whom comes salvation. But while John situates the high-point of redemption in the Word becoming flesh to dwell amongst us, Paul's attention centres upon the saving power of Christ's cross as the key moment in our reconciliation with God.

Before examining in detail the contents of this great christology we should first enquire if it is proper to regard it as a hymn at all, and if so, whether it was composed by St. Paul or simply borrowed by him from another source. Some commentators doubt the propriety of referring to verses 15-20 as a hymn, because "arguments based on rhythm, parallelism and supposed strophic arrangement are precarious when there is no recognisable quantitative metre by which to judge" (Moule). On the other hand a fair case can be made for dividing the passage into two clear-out stanzas, each with its specific theme as follows:

He is the image of the invisible God.
The first-born of all creation;
For in him all things were created
    in heaven and on earth, visible and invisible,
Whether thrones or dominations or principalities or
    authorities
All things were created through him and for him
He is before all things, and in him all things hold
    together.
He is the head of the body, the church;
    He is the beginning, the first-born from the dead,
    That in everything he might be pre-eminent,

For in him the fulness of God was pleased to dwell,
  And through him to reconcile to himself all things
Whether on earth or in heaven
Making peace by the blood of his cross.

The theme of each stanza is announced in its first and final lines. Stanza one deals with the relationship of Christ to the whole of creation and stanza two with his role as redeemer through whom all things but especially his church were reconciled with God. Set out in this form the christology may fairly be called a blank-verse hymn with its own kind of parallelism and balance, even though there is no clearly recognisable rhythm or metre in the individual lines.

Various suggestions are made regarding the origin of this great christology. Some scholars regard it as a well-known early christian hymn, used perhaps for the liturgy of baptism, which Paul simply inserted at this point in his letter. Others have imagined Paul as here adapting a Hellenistic hymn in honour of divine wisdom, in order to produce a strong statement upon the supremacy of Christ. There seems no conclusive reason why these lines might not be an original composition by Paul himself, eager to express the fullness of his faith in Christ, and using for that purpose terminology borrowed from the Wisdom literature of his Jewish background and in part from the Gnostic speculations of his opponents. Whatever their origin, whether borrowed or adapted or freshly composed, these lines about Christ fit perfectly into the structure of the epistle, and even constitute its doctrinal highpoint. We may therefore legitimately interpret the contents of this christology in the light of what Paul has written elsewhere about Jesus.

Our inherited Jewish belief that man is made in the image of God (Gen 1:26; 1 Cor 11:7; Col 3:10) applies in a supereminent way to Christ. He thus forms the living bridge between the transcendent Creator and the visible world. The idea that God projects one uniquely perfect image of himself was already current amongst the Jews at Alexandria where wisdom was called "a reflection of eternal light, a spotless mirror of the working of God, and an image of his goodness" (Wis 7:26). When the early Christians sought a way of describing the unique relationship of Jesus to God, here was a glorious concept already to hand.

The phrase "first-born of all creation" is somewhat ambiguous. While undoubtedly charged with a rich resonance of meaning it could be open to serious misinterpretation. It cannot be intended to locate Christ as *first of all creatures*, in the sense of being included among created things. "First-born," like "image," is closely connected with and taken from the Alexandrian vocabulary of the *Logos* (Word of God). What it affirms is the intimate proximity of Christ to the Father, and his priority to all creation. In other words it declares the absolute pre-existence of the Son. The Arian heretics in the fourth century were mistaken in appealing to this phrase as a proof that Christ was a created being, albeit the highest of creatures. Its significance is rather that he stands in the relation of first-born to all creation, prior to and supreme above it, since Paul goes on to say all things were created through him and for him. First-born should therefore be interpreted in the sense of pre-eminent, an idea that returns in verse 18. In the only other text where Paul refers to Jesus as the first-born it also has overtones of supremacy: God's Son becomes "first-born of many brethren" precisely insofar as they are conformed to his image (Rm 8:29).

"In Him, through Him and for Him" (v.16) – here the supremacy of Christ over creation could not be more plainly stated, thus clarifying the significance of "first-born." The whole universe of things, not only the visible but also the spiritual world, originated through him and tends towards him. It is a vast claim and a profound one, attributing to the person of Christ what the Alexandrian Jewish tradition attributed to the wisdom or word of God. Within the invisible forces subject to Christ, four orders of angelic beings are named (thrones, dominions, principalities, authorities).

Mention of these forces not only heightens the impression of our whole passage. It should be understood in terms of the heresy Paul is here opposing, and hence as *ad hominem* rather than as serious angelology.

It seems fair to assume that the heretical opponents at Colossae were of the type later known as Gnostics. Apparently, they maintained that Christ was only one among superhuman forces with whom men had to reckon. They sharply distinguished matter from spirit, regarding the material world as essentially evil and far estranged from God, the unseen ultimate spirit. Any contact between God and the world required a series of emanations or intermediary beings, a complex celestial hierarchy capable of bridging the gap between pure spirit and impure matter. Correspondingly men could only rise towards union with God through progressive spiritualisation, achieved through that secret knowledge which the Gnostics claimed to possess.

RECONCILIATION AND FIRMNESS.
1:21-23.

> [21] And you, who once were estranged and hostile in mind, doing evil deeds, [22] he has now reconciled in his body of flesh by his death, in order to present you holy and blameless and irreproachable before him, [23] provided that you continue in the faith, stable and steadfast, not shifting from the hope of the gospel which you heard, which has been preached to every creature under heaven, and of which I, Paul, became a minister.

A prominent feature of this epistle is the contrast it makes between the present and the past, so as to highlight for the converts from paganism the great change which faith in Christ has brought into their lives. As he did in Romans (Rom 1:21-32), Paul paints a dark picture (v.21) of their previous pagan existence, a life separated from God

not only through immoral conduct but through the very
cast of their mind and heart. They were "darkened in their
mind, alienated from the life of God" (Eph 4:18).

In happy contrast to their previous alienated condition,
they are now established in peace and friendship with God
(v.22). Whereas already (v.20) the blood and the cross of
Christ were mentioned as a means of this restoration, now a
slightly fuller explanation is given: reconciliation came
through "his body of flesh by his death." By a wonderful
paradox of divine wisdom it was precisely in what united
Christ to our weakness that he restored us. It was through
sharing the limits, the vulnerability and the mortality of our
mortal flesh (Rom 8:3; 2 Cor 5:21; Gal 3:13) that he won us
back from death to life.

He wishes to present us *"holy and blameless and ire-
reproachable."* The redemptive death of Christ should have
moral results in the lives of the faithful. A sacrificial metaphor is employed: Christ wishes to present his faithful as a
blameless sacrifice to God, just as he once offered himself.
In order to benefit from our Lord's sacrifice a Christian must
himself become a pure, unsullied sacrifice to God (Rom
12:1; Phil 2:17). There is no reconciliation without cooperation. Our voluntary, personal union with Christ's offering
of his obedience is essential to the whole process by which
we are saved. "Christ does for us what we could not do for
ourselves; but we must do for our part what he will not do
for us. He offers us to God but it is nonetheless our own
offering too" (Moule).

Development must be accompanied by *stability* (v.23).
The believer looks back gratefully to that unique sacrifice
of Christ in the past by which we are saved; he looks
forward in hope to the final glory that will be his in the
presence of God; but it is in the present moment that he
must forge the link between the already and the not yet,
steadfastly holding firm to the gospel. Next to Christ
Himself, Paul is the greatest exponent of christian perseverance. There can be no true faith without doing the

will of the Father (Mt 7:21) and salvation will depend upon persevering to the end (Mt 10:22). So along with the joyful message of reconciliation comes the sober reminder to be solidly firm, unlike the foolish man who built his house without foundation (Lk 6:49). Though himself intensely active and adaptable to a variety of circumstances ("all things to all men," 1 Cor 9:22) Paul set immense value on the quality of steadfastness in faith (1 Cor 15:58; Gal 1:6; Eph 3:17). Continuing in faith means more, of course, than holding on to intellectual belief; it is keeping faith with God through living out the Gospel message.

To say that the gospel has been preached "to every creature under heaven" is a hyperbolic expression which harmonizes with the theme of the epistle. Just as the cross of Christ has effect for the whole of creation so his gospel reaches out to every creature, and was destined to reach all mankind (Mt 28:19). Although a great start had been made in this by the apostolic preaching, Paul would be the last to claim that every individual person had yet heard the gospel. He uses the hyperbole here (as in 1 Thess 1:8) to underline the universality of the genuine gospel (in contrast to the elitist versions being proposed by the false teachers) and possibly also to imply his belief that the consummation of God's kingdom was not far off (1 Cor 7:29; cf. Mk 13:10). The obvious recipients of gospel preaching are human beings, though "every creature under heaven" carries overtones of cosmic redemption (Rom 8:21).

Why does he interject into this universalist context the mention of his own personal role (v.23)? There is no reason to think that his readers had contested Paul's apostolic status, which is stated so simply in the opening verse of the epistle. His motive can scarcely be self-glorification, for he describes himself as a servant (*diakonos*) and then alludes to his suffering condition. But it was by now second nature to him to remember his role every time he mentioned the gospel. And in fact this personal reference helped to establish the link between him and the Colossians. Their life in the Spirit began when they accepted the gospel, and will continue if, with the help of apostolic encouragement, they can but deepen their grasp of it. Happily for us, the mention of his ministry leads him to a further reflective comment upon the very essence of apostleship.

APOSTOLIC MEDIATION THROUGH SUFFERING. 1:24-29.

> [24]Now I rejoice in my sufferings for your sake, and in my flesh I complete what is lacking in Christ's afflictions for the sake of his body, that is, the church, [25]of which I became a minister according to the divine office which was given to me for you, to make the word of God fully known, [26]the mystery hidden for ages and generations but now made manifest to his saints. [27]To them God chose to make known how great among the Gentiles are the riches of the glory of this mystery, which is Christ in you, the hope of glory. [28]Him we proclaim, warning every man and teaching every man in all wisdom, that we may present every man mature in Christ. [29]For this I toil, striving with all the energy which he mightily inspires within me.

Here is a richly-compressed statement of Paul's understanding of apostleship, as formulated towards the end of his career. In the space of a few verses he gives a glowing account of the Why, the What and the How of authentic ministry. He mentions his vocation, his message and his presence in spirit to the christian people. But perhaps the most notable feature of this passage is the significance he gives to his own sufferings as performing a real mediatory function on behalf of the church.

With a typical paradox, Paul introduces his extraordinary statement about supplementing the passion of Christ (v.24). He had been aware since the time of his conversion that persecutions endured by Christians for their faith united them with the suffering Christ (Acts 9:5). Very soon he experienced this truth in his own flesh through the hardships, imprisonments and beatings endured in his missionary travels (2 Cor 11:23-33 etc), so that he could speak of being crucified with Christ (Gal 2:20) or of sharing the fellowship (*koinonia*) of his sufferings (Phil 3:10). Midway through his apostolic career he had already established the principle that spiritual joy could abound, precisely in the midst of sacrifice: "Whereas we share abundantly in comfort too" (2 Cor 1:5). He had also discerned how such endurance could positively benefit others (2 Cor 1:4; 4:12). Hence the value of patience was twofold, since it furnishes for him a living link both with the Lord and with the faithful. By the time he wrote to the Colossians Paul's viewpoint was so well known that it can be compressed within a couple of pregnant phrases which fit perfectly at this point in the epistle.

Amazingly this passage glows with joy and zeal. He might well have considered his apostolate at an end now that he was imprisoned, with little prospect of release or of being able to take another missionary journey. Instead, he boldly sees himself as having entered a new phase of ministry particularly fruitful for the life of the church. Now his endurance of the pains of old age and the discomforts of prison will be just as effective as his former preaching in bringing about the conversion and perseverance of the faithful. This prospect brings joy to his apostolic heart.

Yet, for all its generosity and its power of personal witness, Paul's statement about fulfilling a ministry for others through suffering (v.24) requires careful under-standing so as not to diminish the unique and all-sufficient power of Christ's cross. The same terms "completing some-thing lacking" occur elsewhere in the epistles for a service lovingly rendered (1 Cor 16:17; Phil 2:30). But what can have been lacking in those redemptive afflictions by which Christ saved us? What could Paul or anybody else supplement or complete?

Augustine points one way out of the difficulty by saying that it was Christ himself who continued to suffer in the person of the Apostle. In this sense everything done in and by the mystical body is but the extension of Christ's activity upon earth (commentary on Psalm 142). This interpretation is somewhat strained, even though the identification of the apostle's sufferings with those of Christ would find close parallels in what he says elsewhere (Gal 2:20; Ph 3:10), completing something that was lacking, the very point at issue in this verse. The best solution seems to be that whereby the sufferings of Christ are considered under two distinct aspects, sacrificial and ministerial:

a) As expiatory sacrifice the passion of Christ was unique, perfect and all-sufficient; here Paul would perfectly agree with the epistle to the Hebrews, that the sacrifice of Christ was "once for all" (Heb 9:26), and cannot be shared by any other "mediator."

b) As ministerial self-denial, the Lord's afflictions must be shared and supplemented by every generation of his church. It is through this process that the faithful are strengthened in their struggle against sin and the costly grace of redemption is brought home to them.

In a striking juxtaposition of images, the Body of Christ draws benefit from what is endured by the flesh of Paul (v.24). The Body is his well-known term for that permanent social and spiritual union which exists between the Lord and his followers. It emphasises the living, growing quality of the church as well as its dependence upon Christ its head. Reference to being able to serve the church leads to still further reflection upon the particular form of his ministry.

The true apostle always remains conscious that the privileged task of preaching has been given to him as a trust, for the benefit of others. He is merely a dispenser of the goodness of God. The overall plan or economy of salvation is from God himself.

Verse 25 lists three significant things about the task (or stewardship, or ministry) which he fulfils in the church:

a) Vocation comes from above by the will of God rather than from any ambition or zeal on the part of the recipient.

b) It is not for the benefit of the apostle himself but for that of his listeners, who through him are called to conversion and salvation. Paul has in mind here specifically his mission to the Gentiles to whom he had been especially sent by Divine Providence.

c) Bringing the gospel message is the apostle's primary task. If properly announced, God's revelation has its own dynamism and effectiveness. Christian teachers and preachers must have quiet confidence in the word of God and be content to sow it like a good seed, trusting that God will make it fruitful in the hearts of the hearers (1 Cor 3:7). The core of their message will be Jesus Christ himself, as the next three verses make clear.

To state that God's mystery has been "made manifest to the saints" (v.26) encapsulates a most important aspect of christianity, namely that ours is a revealed religion. The "mystery" is the divine plan of salvation, kept secret from all until the appropriate moment for its worldwide announcement in "the fullness of time" (Eph 1:10). There were at that time many religious societies which offered secret teaching to their initiate members while concealing their mysteries from the outside world. The Christian mystery is of a different kind. It remained God's secret plan until the coming of Christ, but now in the era of the church it is an open secret proclaimed to everyone. Of course, not all those who hear the christian message accept it or live by it (cf. Rom 10:18-21). But Paul here concentrates upon the happy lot of those who *do* receive and treasure it: their faith shows them to be God's chosen ones. Many of them are "Gentiles," converts from paganism like most of the faithful at Colossae. Striving to help them appreciate what they have received, he piles enthusiastic phrase upon phrase, to show "how great are the riches of the glory of this mystery."

Ultimately, the great revelation turns out to be not a doctrine but a person (v.27). The mystery revealed is Jesus Christ the crucified and risen Lord, now living among his faithful followers everywhere, Saviour of the Gentiles no less than of the Jews. This personal, living contact with Our Lord, which Paul usually called being *in Christ* (1:2; 2:6), but here more powerfully termed *Christ in you* (compare Rom 8:10; 2 Cor 13:5; Gal 4:19), gives to the faithful a dynamic hope of eternal life. Their bond with the living Lord here and now gives them confidence of sharing a fuller life with him in the future. Here as in Romans 8:18 "glory" refers to that fuller revelation which will be given at the time of Christ's return to those who already possess him and are possessed by him in faith.

In the light of what has already been said about the person of Christ, it is no wonder that he should be accepted by Christians as the heart and centre of religious wisdom. But this verse also seems to hint at the existence of other contrary teachings which offered a different kind of wisdom to the elite, by mingling Christ with other intermediary powers—a current which Paul attacks broadside in the next chapter. Far from being a new, esoteric knowledge reserved to some initiate elect, the knowledge of Christ is open to every man and is the way towards religious maturity for all. To people hankering after some more exciting philosophy to blend with their simple christian faith, Paul says in effect: the fullness of wisdom is to be found in Christ, in whom are hid all the treasures of wisdom and knowledge (cf. 2:3). Christ is proclaimed in two ways—by warning and teaching words related to each other as repentance is to faith (cf. Acts 20:21); people must first be warned of the need for conversion, then instructed in the faith.

The final purpose of all apostolic effort is to bring people to God, as a pleasing sacrifice in his sight (v.28). As in

Romans 12:1 (and in verse 22 above) the verb "to present" has sacrificial overtones and implies divine acceptance. Just as he prays for their growth in wisdom, understanding and endurance (1:10-11) so he can hope that their christian life will be finally fully mature and ready for the eternal joy of God's presence.

Paul's mention of his toil (v.29) offers a striking and "typically christian combination of human effort and divine succour" (Moule). Helping people to develop as full members of Christ's body, which was the *raison d'etre* for all his missionary journeyings, now continued to give him a motive for living during his imprisonment. While his "toil" and "striving" (favourite terms for the apostolate) were now restricted, they remained important. He could still help by letters and messages from prison, by praying for his beloved converts and particularly by accepting on their behalf those ministerial sufferings which preached, more effectively than words, his faith in Christ. Such endurance is possible only when we rely not on ourselves but on God at work within us (cf. 2 Cor 1:9; Phil 2:13).

THE ORIGINS OF PAUL'S MYSTERY AND WISDOM LANGUAGE

We have seen how Paul twice refers to a "mystery," which was once hidden but is now revealed (1:26), and whose content is the indwelling of Christ among the Gentiles (1:27). It is interesting to enquire from what source he drew this notion of a mystery revealed, and what background best helps to explain what he meant by it.

Rudolf Bultmann, an outstanding exponent of Paul's thought, had no hesitation in maintaining that the apostle often borrowed terminology from Gnosticism and from the Hellenistic mystery religions. In his *Theology of the New Testament* (SCM edition, 1955), he suggests that Paul had already appropriated these concepts during his pre-christian years in the Hellenistic city of Tarsus, and that the form of Christianity he adopted was one already deeply impregnated with Greek religious ideas (I, p.187). Accordingly, his understanding of christian initiation through baptism into the dying and rising of Christ was indebted to the contemporary mystery religions (I, p.298). Following Bultmann's lead, many have imagined that Paul's use of the language of mystery, and particularly of the notion of indwelling in Christ the Saviour, derived from a pagan Greek source rather than having its roots in the Semitic origins of the Church. The apostle himself would be the archetypal syncretist, among the first to blend non-Jewish ideas with the tradition deriving from Jesus.

A contrary viewpoint has been gaining ground in the past twenty years—due in large part to the additional knowledge we have gained about the complexity of Jewish beliefs, through the Dead Sea Scrolls. In an outstanding study of the Semitic Concept of Mystery (*C.B.Q.* 1958, 417-443, later published in expanded form by Fortress Press, Philadelphia, 1968), Raymond Brown was able to link St. Paul's mystery terminology with that of the Old Testament Wisdom literature, and with ideas current among the Essenes at Qumran. Brown's theory has since been buttressed by the work of other scholars, so that nowadays "it is difficult to believe that Paul could have deliberately borrowed from any source extraneous to Judaism" (A.T. Hanson: *Studies in Paul's Techniques and Theology*, London, 1974, p.211).

In support of the Semitic source, the argument runs briefly thus: Paul totally accepted the primitive christian kerygma that everything concerning Jesus happened "according to the Scriptures" (1 Cor 15:3-4). This led him to a painstaking search of these (Old Testament) Scriptures for whatever foreshadowings they gave of Christ's role and significance—first, concerning his redemptive work as suffering Servant, but also regarding whatever hints they offered about his divine identity as united to and yet distinct from Yahweh, Creator and Lord of Israel. In the portrayal of Wisdom as a personified being, eternally and creatively coming forth from God, Paul found his most fruitful model for understanding the personal identity of Christ. Having discerned the concept of pre-existent Wisdom active in the history of Israel, the early Christians were enabled—even on Semitic background alone—to transfer the name "Lord" (which for Greek-speaking Jews was the equivalent of Yahweh) from being the exclusive prerogative of the Father and apply it also to the Son. This process culminates in the doctrine of Colossians "where the identification of Christ with the creative Wisdom is quite explicit and we have a christology as advanced as that of the fourth gospel" (Hanson).

Having recognized Christ as the incarnate Wisdom of God, it was not a long step to begin to speak of him as the revelation of God's Mystery. In the Semitic literature upon which Paul was able to draw—not only the later Old Testament books but also the "Pseudepigrapha" (Enoch, IV Ezra, II and III Baruch) and the Qumran writings—the notion of divine mysteries was already current. God was thought of as deliberating within Himself, or with the heavenly court, to enact the government of creation, or to plan the destiny of man. Nor are these divine mysteries kept always secret from men, since the notion of revelation is also intertwined with them: God reveals his secrets to his servants the prophets (Amos 3:7), and it is characteristic of the wicked that "they knew not the secrets (*mysteria*) of God" (Wis 2:22). Similarly in the non-biblical Jewish writings there is quite frequent mention of secrets and mysteries whether of good or evil, the knowledge of which is granted to those whose minds are attuned to religious wisdom. At the end of his quite detailed review of the Semitic material, Raymond Brown could say that "despite the fact that we possess only a fraction of the Jewish literature available to St. Paul, we believe that—considering the variety and currency of the concept of divine mysteries in Jewish thought—Paul could have written everything he did about *mysterion* whether or not he ever encountered the pagan mystery-religions. Mystery was a part of the theological equipment of the Jews who came to Christ" (p.69).

It is well to recognize at the same time that Paul must have been aware of the popularity of "mystery" language in the Greek culture which was part of the Colossians' background, and which was also current in his native Tarsus. Furthermore, the late Old Testament writers and particularly the author of the book of Wisdom, show some familiarity with the language of the Greek mystery religions "which would be the common possession of Alexandrians in the period just before Christ" (Brown, p.12). Hence, though he appears to have exaggerated the point, we cannot totally dismiss Bultmann's contention that Paul's mystery language for the revelation of Christ derives in part at least from pagan Greek sources. In a minor and totally acceptable sense, the apostle was himself a syncretist when faced with the challenge of theological growth!

A SPECIAL KIND OF ENCOURAGEMENT.
2:1-7.

Paul's power of encouragement derives in large part from the candour in telling others of his personal feelings towards them. Even modern Christians whose own emotions are so carefully veiled beneath a mask of reserve or inhibition can hardly help responding to the animation with which he tells his friends how dear they are to him and how much he is concerned for their progress. His very life-style, of course, testified to the genuineness of that affection. Here as elsewhere his pastoral concern is proven by personal hardships borne on behalf of his people. Concern which results in endurance is genuine coin and offers the only worthwhile basis from which to appeal to others for a like perseverance. Knowing themselves deeply cherished by such a pastor they are encouraged to stick to their initial commitment.

2 For I want you to know how greatly I strive for you, and for those at Laodicea, and for all who have not seen my face, ²that their hearts may be encouraged as they are knit together in love, to have all the riches of assured understanding and the knowledge of God's mystery, of Christ, ³in whom are hid all the treasures of wisdom and knowledge. ⁴I say this in order that no one may delude you with beguiling speech. ⁵For though I am absent in body, yet I am with you in spirit, rejoicing to see your good order and the firmness of your faith in Christ.

⁶As therefore you received Christ Jesus the Lord, so live in him, ⁷rooted and built up in him and established in the faith, just as you were taught, abounding in thanksgiving.

He wants them to know how he feels (v.1). There is no hint here of that misguided spirituality which loves mankind but cannot stand people. While the whole world was his parish, he professes special concern for the people at Colossae and their neighbours in Laodicea. Although he had not yet visited either community, he takes the first opportunity to write so as to counter the dangers which threatened them. It was the best he could do in the circumstances, until after his release, when he would surely have visited Colossae and Laodicea on the way to visit his old friend Philemon (Philem 22). Since the two towns were only a dozen miles apart, Paul had good reason to fear that any church trouble in one of them could easily spread to the other. Therefore he orders that his letter to the Colossians should be read out also in the church at Laodicea and vice versa (4:16). There is an interesting hypothesis that the letter from Laodicea might be identical with the epistle to the Ephesians, "an expanded synthesis of the new insights attained by Paul in reacting to the crisis at Colossae" (Murphy-O'Connor).

The kind of maturity Paul wishes for them (v.2) is substantially the same as that for which he had earlier prayed (1:9-12). They are to have courage, harmony and a firm understanding of the christian truth—all three being needed if they were to resist superficial attractions of a new doctrine which was being proposed with beguiling speech. They must stand united both in love and in the truth. For Paul, indeed, there could be no true spiritual understanding without that love which is the bond of perfection (3:14). The impending danger from false religious teachers must be met by a united community, firm in their understanding of and devotion to Christ.

If Christ is the ultimate unveiling of God's secret plan for man's salvation, then we need look no further than him for the wisdom and knowledge that we require (v.3). But why does Paul refer to this treasure as hidden, now that he has described the mystery as manifest to the saints (1:26)? Perhaps he wishes to echo a phrase from Isaiah, "I will give you the treasures of darkness and the hoards of secret places" (Is 45:3). His more likely motive is that the term "hidden" was already being used with reference to secret, grandiose knowledge claimed by the false teachers. In effect, Paul declares that if there is any "secret" knowledge it is to be found in Christ. That fullness of wisdom which the Jew sought in the law, and the Greek in his philosophy, was available to the Christian in the person of Jesus Christ. The faithful should cling to this conviction no matter what beguiling claims to the contrary they might hear.

The epistle has consisted so far almost entirely in a positive statement, reminding the Colossians of what they had already heard and praising them for their belief in Jesus Christ. Its tone will soon shift, to become a frontal assault upon the danger hanging over the community; but before this change to the withering tone of polemics, Paul brings the encouraging section of his epistle to an admirable and characteristic conclusion (2:5-7). In these three verses we meet at least five recognizable elements of his pastoral style:

a) He is present to his readers in spirit. Even though absent in body, his affection and concern for his communities form a bridge that transcends the barriers of space (1 Thess 2:17; 1 Cor 5:3; Phil 1:7).

b) He expresses contentment with their progress to date, being careful to praise before offering correction. (In view of what he will say in the polemical section, some would regard his compliment in v.5 about their good order and firmness as pure diplomacy, a gesture of goodwill, or an expression of hope rather than of assurance).

c) He reminds them of their initial acceptance of Christ (cf. 1 Thess 2:13; 1 Cor 15:1; Gal 1:9; Phil 4:9). This reference to the traditional formulation of faith tacitly rejects any contrary attempts at remodeling the christian message.

d) He expects them at the same time to develop in their adherence to the faith, being rooted in Christ and *built up* in him—(twin metaphors that are already found in 1 Cor 3:9 "You are God's field, God's building"). For Paul, christian life is not a static firmness but a living pilgrimage, solidly rooted yet always growing. This notion of continued growth is particularly remarkable in the captivity epistles (Col 1:10; 2:10; 3:10; Eph 1:18; 2:21; Phil 3:12-15).

e) He urges thanksgiving, a theme so frequent in this epistle as to be almost a refrain (1:12; 3:15-17; 4:2). It expresses joyful appreciation of the gifts of God and especially of the supreme gift of salvation through Jesus Christ. The believer who has this spirit of gratitude will not easily be shifted by the latest fad or fashion. Such is the positive basis from which Paul can launch his attack upon the false doctrine which threatened the peace and the stability of the Colossian church.

ERROR VERSUS TRUTH.
2:8-23.

It is in this polemical section that we learn what was really troubling St. Paul and that he "gets down to the real business of the letter" (Murphy-O'Connor). He makes it clear that some were propounding a spurious religious philosophy which was not in accordance with Christ. Of course the great concentration upon Christ in the first portion of the letter already suggests something of what was afoot. Now however he tackles the problems squarely and openly. Since the fullness of the believer's life comes from Christ, Paul rejects outright any notion that other intermediaries were needed for man's salvation, or that any auxiliary disciplines or asceticism were required apart from normal christian living. The three components of the section set out the contrast between the bondage of man-made traditions and the divine liberty of redemption, granted us by the Father through Jesus Christ.

OUR CANCELLED BONDAGE.
2:8-15.

[8]See to it that no one makes a prey of you by philosophy and empty deceit, according to human tradition, according to the elemental spirits of the universe, and not according to Christ. [9]For in him the whole fulness of deity dwells bodily, [10]and you have come to fulness of life in him, who is the head of all rule and authority. [11]In him also you were circumcised with a circumcision made without hands, by putting off the body of flesh in the circumcision of Christ: [12]and you were buried with him in baptism, in which you were also raised with him through faith in the working of God, who raised him from the dead. [13]And you, who were dead in trespasses and the uncircumcision of your flesh, God made alive together with him, having forgiven us all our trespasses, [14]having canceled the bond which stood against us with its legal demands; this he set aside, nailing it to the cross. [15]He disarmed the principalities and powers and made a public example of them, triumphing over them in him.

The motif underlying verse 8, and repeated in vv.16-23, is that the Colossians were in danger of being spiritually kidnapped and enslaved by the eloquent purveyors of superstition. When Paul equates philosophy with empty deceit, it is simply a way of belittling the vaunted wisdom of his opponents and not a rejection of rational thought as such. Many in his day would have claimed the name "philosophy" for their speculations concerning super-human powers which controlled human affairs, along with the patent remedies by which man could supposedly come to terms with them. This welter of speculation was interwoven with the myths and legends of the ancient world; the kind specifically referred to here was that based on the "elemental spirits" of the universe. This phrase may mean either elementary worldly notions or the ele-mental beings which control the world—cosmic powers of some kind. The latter is its most likely sense here, since the personification of the cosmic elements would pose a serious threat to the unique mediation of Jesus Christ as man's Saviour and Lord. Many of the pagans, and not a few heretical Jews, thought of the heavenly bodies as having a controlling influence on the fate of men. (This superstition still thrives today when millions consult their horoscopes, half-believing that their lives are governed by the movement of the stars). All such beliefs Paul rejects as mere man-made tradition, fallacious, misleading and opposed to the true, divine guarantee of salvation through the cross.

To offset any claim that these elemental spirits had anything worthwhile to offer as a supplement to the christian gospel, Paul returns to his insistence upon the uniqueness and universal significance of Christ (v.9). The Christ-hymn had already affirmed that the fullness of God dwelt in Him. Now he adds the evocative but puzzling adverb "bodily," for which at least five interpretations have been offered. It could mean: (a) in one body, not distributed through a hierarchy of beings; (b) expressing itself through the body of Christ, the church; (c) in reality, not in mere appearance; (d) in its very essence; (e) in a bodily, incarnate form. With Lightfoot and others we prefer this fifth interpretation, referring to the human body of Christ. Paul has already said that the fullness of divinity belonged to Christ from the beginning. This fullness remained with Christ even when he emptied himself by taking the form of a slave (Phil 2:7). Thus the bodily indwelling of divinity in Christ is the equivalent to St. John's concept of the Word-made-flesh (Jn 1:14). Paul resists as stoutly as does John any docetist trend which would refuse to accept the reality of incarnation or would baulk at the idea of God taking upon himself our human flesh.

Disciples have come to *fullness of life* in him (v.10). Corresponding to the completeness of divinity within Christ himself is the completeness of salvation which he acquired for his faithful followers. Positively, Paul wants to affirm the rich heritage of life that is granted through Christ, through whom the Father gives us all things (Rom 8:32). Negatively, he wants to rule out the claim raised by some at Colossae that an extra degree of spiritual maturity was available through other religious rites and beliefs. For if Christ is head of all rule and authority, no other fulfilment is available apart from him. The next three verses pursue this idea by harping upon the radical re-birth which is entitled in christian baptism. After such total purification from former ways, it would be foolish to revert back to the "empty deceit" of non-christian practises.

What Paul means by associating baptism and circumcision (vv.11-13) is clear enough in its context, though the wording is tortuous and somewhat obscure. Circumcision—the removal of the foreskin performed on all male Jews eight days after their birth—initiated one into the covenanted people of God. But now baptism has replaced it, as the new, spiritual, interior initiation. Paul has used this equivalence elsewhere to explain how the baptized faithful become the true Israel, descendants of Abraham (Rom 2:25-29 etc). Though he had successfully fought to prevent the imposition of physical circumcision upon his converts, he continued to value the deep symbolism of that ancient Jewish rite since it prefigured the baptismal ideal of dying and rebirth by the putting off of a portion of one's flesh. For Jews and those within the influence of their culture, that ritual would always evoke the idea of initiation, reconciliation, transformation—precisely the effects now achieved by baptism. The phrase *circumcision of Christ* may be interpreted here as a synonym for his passion, that total stripping-off of his physical body which inaugurated our new, baptismal circumcision "not made with hands" (cf. Mk 14:58). Paul might even have intended it simply as a cryptic equivalent for christian baptism, hence as "the circumcision [brought in] by Christ," through which the old, sensual self is cut away and put to death. In either sense, it is one of the phrases "whereby Paul extends the death of Christ to the dying of the individual" (John A. Robinson: *The Body*, p.46). The baptized have undergone a profound change of state, described first as "putting off" the sensual self or "burial" with Christ, and then as being "raised" or "made alive" with him. What this means is that they must leave behind their previous worldly practises and thought-patterns, "cut off as completely as the particle of skin in circumcision, and no longer part of us" (Murphy-O'Connor).

To avoid any presumptuous reliance upon baptism as though it were a magical rite whose effectiveness was purely automatic, Paul mentions the correlative of personal faith in the working of God (v.12). Interior renewal depends not only upon the objective gift of God (the passion of Christ, applied to individual lives through baptism) but also upon our subjective acceptance (the free, personal decision of those who receive this gift and live accordingly). Baptism and faith blend as closely together as the dying and rising of Jesus. What Paul envisages is the adult baptism of persons well-instructed in the faith and deliberate in their option for a new way of life. Through faith, their symbolic immersion in water became a real incorporation into Christ.

Forgiveness is an integral part of this renewal. Just as in the previous chapter (1:22) here once again Paul mentions the essentially moral nature of redemption (v.13). New, spiritual life can come only where sin is forgiven. The former life-style of the Colossians—like the unregenerate state of everyman—was morally uncircumcized, removed from God's good pleasure, hence a state of spiritual death. By a mighty paradox, our release from this state of death comes through participation in the death of Christ, which cancels the hold of past sins and then "makes alive" through the power of his resurrection. We are thus allowed to begin afresh, in accordance with the life-giving will of God. The word "to forgive" (cf. Rom 8:32; Lk 7:42-43) contains the notion of generous grace freely given in advance of man's response. Fully aware of his own need for God's mercy, Paul has shifted from "you" to "we," thereby situating himself within the ranks of the forgiven.

The passage ends with a picturesque description of how this freedom was achieved: the cancellation of our bondage (vv.14-15). All great preaching is rooted in vivid imagery drawn from life. Where Jesus was supreme in fashioning parables based on village and country life, Paul's preference was for rapid metaphors taken from the bustling ethos of the city. Here we find no less than three of these assembled in collage: a legal bond, public crucifixion and triumphant procession. The overall effect is to show that Jesus "has done all that can be done, and that there is no need to bring in any other intermediaries for the full salvation of men" (Barclay).

a) The debtor's bond: This graphic image conjures up the plight of one whose faults are staring him in the face, like a contract brandished before its acknowledged signatory. Our sinfulness is just as plain as a documentary pledge, upon which is written our plain duty towards God. For a

Jew, this was enshrined in the Mosaic Law, which he revered but did not faithfully observe (cf. Ex 24:7; Rm 2:17-24). For the Gentile, it was the interior dictate of conscience since "what the law requires is written on their hearts" (Rom 2:15). In both cases, men stood accused of defaulting. "There was a sense of being in debt and of never catching up with one's payments" (Thompson). Then Christ stepped in to wipe out the debtor's bond as writing is erased from a blackboard, so that we start again with a clean slate. This is no denial that we have sinned—of that, nobody was more conscious than the former Pharisee from Tarsus—but an act of gratuitous mercy, to expunge the crushing catalogue of human guilt.

b) Nailed to the cross: To further dramatize this total cancellation of our bond, Paul envisages it fastened publicly upon Christ's saving cross. The image might derive from a method of abrogating decrees by running a nail through them in some public place—though there is no clear evidence for this. Its significance here is that our sinful burden is lifted precisely through the power of the cross. The same nails which fastened Christ have set man's heart and conscience free.

c) The triumph of Christ: A third vivid picture flashes through Paul's mind, illustrating how absurd it would be to rely upon the mediation of cosmic powers. These are now totally overcome and led in captive procession, as a victorious Roman general would march his prisoners through the streets in triumph. The subject of the verb "to triumph" can be Christ, or God acting through him. Continuing the paradox of the passion, it was through the apparent helplessness of crucifixion that Jesus disarmed those malignant forces hostile to man's welfare. He stripped them off as he emptied himself—so that his cross of shame becomes in reality a victory chariot, "leading captivity captive" (Eph 4:8). Paul insists on the public and final nature of this victory. Insofar as Christians perceive the crucifixion in this light they are spared from any abject fear regarding the influence of evil powers, or of any need to placate them.

THE WRONG RECIPE.
2:16-19.

> [16]Therefore let no one pass judgment on you in questions of food and drink or with regard to a festival or a new moon or a sabbath. [17]These are only a shadow of what is to come; but the substance belongs to Christ. [18]Let no one disqualify you, insisting on self-abasement and worship of angels, taking his stand on visions, puffed up without reason by his sensuous mind, [19]and not holding fast to the Head, from whom the whole body, nourished and knit together through its joints and ligaments, grows with a growth that is from God.

This passage begins with an emphatic "therefore." Now that he has rebutted the major premise on which the false teachers relied (i.e. superstitious fear of the evil powers), Paul can proceed to an attack upon the details of their ritualistic and ascetical programme. He had always upheld the principle of interior liberty in regard to the use of eating and drinking (cf. Rom 14:1-4; 1 Cor 8:8-9; 1 Tim 4:3; 5:23). Here he defends it vigorously against the set of unhelpful, inane prohibitions being urged by Jews of a Gnostic tendency. While the precise structures imposed by the "puffed up" teachers are not named, they are grouped under headings: observance of fixed times, of particular foods, worship of angels and self-abasement (fasting). Even if such rituals possessed some religious value in the centuries before Christ, now they are but "shadow" compared to the "substance"—that one perfect sacrifice by which we are redeemed. Heb 10:5 draws a similar contrast between the old, ineffective, Jewish sacrificial system and the one final achievement.

The "disqualification" image (v.16) derives from the athletic arena where an umpire could declare a contender to have infringed the rules or to be running on the wrong track. In similar fashion, the ascetic ritualists presumed to arbitrate the rules of religious practise and "declared the Pauline competitor to be no genuine competitor in the race at all" (Moule). The apostle strikes back by ridiculing their pretended visions as illusory. He even brands their fundamental outlook as corrupt, since to place so much emphasis upon external regulations only manifests a "fleshly" or sensual mind. Even their angel-worship was sensuous, compared with the truly spiritual worship initiated by faith in Christ.

"The head from whom the whole body grows"—this phrase is inserted to provide yet another affirmation of Christ's central role. It says, in effect: "if you want to think about body, discipline, nourishment and growth—here's the christian key to these: Hold fast to Christ. He (the head) will provide us (the body) with all the guidance and power we need, to grow towards God."

We should be careful not to read the above passage and the one that follows as though Paul himself were opposed to a certain spiritual restraint regarding material things and their moderate, disciplined use. "The distinction is not between spiritual and material, but between matters of ultimate concern and trivialities; and these must be defined with reference to Christ. The practises and regulations proposed by the false teachers were conceived as having a value in and of themselves, and as such Paul vigorously repudiates them. He is not opposed to external observances as such but to a materialistic kind of superstitious ritualism" (Murphy-O'Connor).

EXCURSUS: PAUL'S TREATMENT OF HERESY.

The polemical content of chapter 2 draws attention to a problem that remains as vital today as in the Church of the first century, namely the need for criteria to distinguish between ideas which are heretical (incompatible with faith, therefore to be rejected) and those which are positive theological developments (doctrinally enriching, hence to be welcomed). Those speculations, prescriptions and prohibitions attacked by Paul provide a clear example of early Christian heresy. While their roots lay outside the Church, these notions were eagerly assimilated by some members of the Colossian community, who prized them as a new dimension to the faith. Theirs was a cumulative approach to religion, adding material from every available source so as to improve their chances of coming in contact with God; hence their attempt to mingle with the original apostolic faith all the fashionable currents of devotion then favoured by their pagan and Jewish contemporaries.

On a positive and sympathetic assessment, this effort might have been welcomed as creative adaptation to the trend of those times. Had not Paul himself attempted to state his faith in the categories of his rivals and opponents at Corinth, where he sought to be "all things to all men" (1 Cor 9:22)? Was he not willing to quote their slogans, such as "all things are lawful for me" and "all of us possess knowledge" (6:12; 8:1)? But whereas this kind of dialogue seemed fruitful in the Corinthian situation, he discerned in the Colossian heresy a more serious and direct threat to the faith. Whatever their surface attraction, the views being propagated at Colossae were incapable of proper integration into the gospel message; they were "not according to Christ" (2:8), and should be vigorously resisted. This reaction prepares the way for the even more intransigent rejection of heresy which we meet in the Pastoral Epistles, where false teaching is to be silenced, without argument (1 Tim 1:3-7; 1:19-20; 4:1-3; 6:3-5; 6:20; 2 Tim 3:5-9; Ti 1:13; 3:9). At the same time we should admit the indirect benefit conferred on the Church by the teachers of error at Colossae, since they elicited from St. Paul his highest christological statement. It would appear that faith occasionally needs the stimulus of heretical opinion in order to produce its own fullest expression by way of reaction. This indeed has been the historical experience of the Church, especially in its conciliar definitions.

It is well to recall the kind of religious situation to which Colossians responds, in view of its relevance for the quest of theological orthodoxy today. Despite obvious differences separating the first century from our own, there are some unmistakable parallels with today's situation. The prevailing religious atmosphere then (as now) was marked by a spirit of insecurity, experimental questing, and pluralism.

The major factor contributing to this situation in Paul's time was the recent and rapid spread of the Roman empire. Among the conquered peoples around the Mediterranean, this fact demanded considerable social and cultural readjustment. It had rocked the ancient religious traditions of the old city-states in Greece and Asia Minor, whose local divinities had proven powerless to withstand the invading legions. These forcibly Romanized peoples had lost many of their old securities along with their independence, and felt the need for some new creed which could stabilize and fortify the individual spirit within the new, imperial world-scene. One among the many religious currents offering to fulfil this need was the christian gospel, which benefited greatly from the novel freedom of travel provided by the political unity and engineering genius of Rome. Yet the very ease of communications that allowed the gospel to travel so quickly from Palestine to Spain also posed the serious problem of maintaining the faith in its purity, alongside competing currents and creeds. "In the absence of any generally recognized religion, the field was open to every kind of belief. All over the empire people were at work trying to create new religions out of different combinations of the old" (Hendriksen). Furthermore, the Roman world showed deep respect for Greek philosophy, whose terms and concepts were therefore being assimilated to a greater or lesser extent by all religious systems, including the christian faith as formulated by St. Paul. Accordingly, whoever was in search of wisdom, peace of mind, moral guidance, religious insight and salvation could find many a plausible creed competing for his allegiance. Such a variety of vibrant religious options has scarcely been available at any period since then, until the modern age of worldwide communications and cultural pluralism.

One very understandable response to such variety was (and is) the desire to blend together the most attractive elements from the various systems and form one's own "syncretist" outlook. Where religion is regarded primarily as an insurance cover against the forces of evil and of death, people are apt to adopt a whole range of superstitious remedies offered from the most incompatible sources, whether because of persuasive speaking or on the personal recommendation of their friends. The syncretism which involves heresy must not be confused with that lesser and legitimate mixing of optional devotions within the christian tradition. Paul himself promoted free personal discernment among the many claims and suggestions which might be made: "Test all things, holding fast to what is good" (1 Thes 5:21). Without a responsible discernment made on the basis of mature Christian faith, there was every danger—both then and now—of sowing weeds among the wheat by inserting into the community items that were fundamentally alien to Christ's gospel.

On the question of how the weeds could be definitively recognized from the wheat, some (like Walter Bauer: *Orthodoxy and Heresy in Early Christianity*) have denied that this ever happened in Paul's time, since in that first generation the gospel had only the simplest form and was capable of expression under almost any set of contemporary concepts. In that brief period before the development of a fixed orthodoxy, no heresy—strictly speaking—was possible. Bauer held that the earliest clear condemnation of heresy came towards the end of the first century, with the Pastoral Epistles, fictitiously attributed to St. Paul but lacking in his liberal theological spirit. According to Bauer's view, Paul himself would hardly have understood the distinction later made in the Catholic Church between orthodoxy and heresy. This opinion, however, is somewhat eccentric in the light of Paul's total rejection of the errors at Colossae. The apostle's stance shows all the signs of a firm Christological orthodoxy, against which other trends could be measured and found wanting. Quite categorically, Paul brands the "beguiling speech" and "empty deceit" of his opponents as ideas arising from a misguided, "sensuous mind," and at variance with the true tradition about Jesus, Lord and Saviour. Hence his appeal to them to remain "rooted and built up in Christ, just as you were taught" (2:7).

While Bauer and others may have understated Paul's position regarding the orthodox expression of faith, it is surely mistaken to go to the opposite extreme, and insist so unilaterally upon the received formulae that any new or experimental attempts to explain Christ in new categories would be suspect of heresy. Conservative Catholicism has more than once in the past century seen the harassment of creative theologians who were sincerely attempting to present Christ in modern language, adapted to a mentality shaped by science, technical advances and existentialist value-judgments. The ideas of Teilhard de Chardin, Henri de Lubac and other writers from the *nouvelle vague* in France during the 1940's and 50's may now have been rehabilitated, but the danger of excessive zeal in the detection of heresy is still real enough. Paul's intransigence in opposing the Colossian error must be balanced by his own constant effort to find new and better formulations for the faith he had received. In doctrine no less than in morals, the apostle sought for authentic development: "not that I have already obtained this or am already perfect . . . I strain forward to what lies ahead, I press on toward the goal" (Phil 3:12-14). In his own example he epitomizes the perfect combination of creativity and conservatism that must always shape theology within the pilgrim church.

What criterion did St. Paul use for judging that the ascetical trend at Colossae, with its devotion to the elemental spirits and its particular forms of self-abasement, was the wrong kind of syncretism? How did he know that it spelled a distortion rather than a legitimate development of Christian doctrine? The answer is surely that this trend conflicted with the vital core of the gospel, the centrality of Jesus Christ as our mediator and only saviour. Even though a fully worked out doctrinal statement about the nature and function of Christ did not yet exist, his role as redeeming Lord was sufficiently understood to warrant the rejection of other intermediaries like those being promoted by the beguiling speakers at Colossae. While there was, certainly, room for fuller development in the theology of redemption, it could not be in that direction!

Having recognized the heretical error for what it was, Paul shows great energy in opposing it, both authoritatively and persuasively. His style in dealing with the crisis is a model of responsible leadership. Far from attempting to silence his opponents with a merely juridical condemnation, he exposes the danger of enslavement which was concealed in their error. First, however, he sets out to confirm the genuine faith of the Colossian community by a strong, masterful presentation of the person of Christ. His pedagogy consists of accentuating the positive before undermining the negative. Treating his readers as intelligent adults, he wins them back to orthodoxy more by persuasion than by threat, and all within a tone of loving concern for their further development. Additional power is lent to his argument by the current of sacrificial, personal witness which underlies it (1:24; 2:1). From such an apostle, imprisoned for the faith, admonition carries sufficient weight to counter even the most fashionable of heresies. We cannot, of course, expect from every prelate the same moral persuasiveness shown by St. Paul; yet in the great pastoral wisdom which he displays, is there not an ideal to be aimed at whenever a church leader seeks to respond effectively to heretical influence? It is significant also that the apostle denounces the erroneous views without naming the actual persons propagating them. "Let no one delude you, make prey of you, or pass judgment on you" (2:4,8,16)—this fashion of condemning the sin rather than the sinner continues in the Church as the way best calculated to restore good order while trying to avoid excluding anyone from the community of the faith.

TRUE AND FALSE SUBMISSION.
2:20-23.

> [20]If with Christ you died to the elemental spirits of the universe, why do you live as if you still belonged to the world? Why do you submit to regulations, [21]"Do not handle, Do not taste, Do not touch" [22](referring to things which all perish as they are used), according to human precepts and doctrines? [23]These have indeed an appearance of wisdom in promoting rigour of devotion and self-abasement and severity to the body, but they are of no value in checking the indulgence of the flesh.

The essential danger of rigid and superstitious regulations is that they actually fix our attention upon the material world, whereas we should be holding fast to Christ. Instead of attempting to appease the "elemental spirits" Christians should ignore them, having "died" to them in baptism. Now that they belong to one master only, they are "in the world but not of it," i.e. not dominated by its fears, threats and selfish principles. Paul brands all the vaunted asceticism of his opponents as merely human precepts and doctrines. However impressive these may seem, they fail to help us gain that fundamental liberty from sin (deep-rooted in "the flesh"), which can only come through submitting in faith to Christ.

The way is now clear for the statement of positive morality which flows from genuine, lifegiving submission.

III. THE MORAL SECTION:
Living the Risen Life (3:1-4:6)

IN ANY WELL-DEVELOPED SYSTEM of theology, doctrine will receive logical priority over the moral requirements which flow from it. Paul consistently observes this proper sequence. Even though he never sets out explicitly to write a systematic treatise on Christian living, his basic pattern remains the movement from "is" to "ought," so that his ethical and moral guidance clearly derives from the central dogmatic insights of the faith. Accordingly, his concentration upon matters of behaviour tends to come in the latter portion of the epistles (e.g. 1 Thes 4-5; 2 Thes 3; Phil 2-4; Gal 5 etc.). This pattern is particularly evident in Colossians, the second half of which draws out the ethical conclusions from what was stated in the first.

The major doctrinal focus upon the person of Christ in the first two chapters receives its logical follow-through in the second half, where Christ provides the mainspring of truly Christian living. Just as he was mediator of redemption through his cross, he now remains the unitive and uplifting force binding his community together with the virtues of hope, love and perseverance. This underlying motif gives a satisfying harmony to the whole epistle, allowing us to see the basically simple outline of the essential Christian message, no matter how complex the issues to which we must apply it. It is through the Lord Jesus that we are reconciled with God (1:20) and in his name that we in turn must try to make our grateful response, giving thanks to the Father through him (3:17).

Within the moral section itself, an elementary logical order may be discerned, whereby the appeal moves from the universal to the particular, from principle to practice.

Thus the fundamental principle of conversion (3:1-4) leads on to practical guidance contrasting the new with the old (3:5-10); the vestments of harmony (3:12-14) illustrate the ideal of mankind reunited (3:11); and—somewhat loosely at least—the passage upon domestic relationship (3:18-4:1) can be regarded as a corollary to that fullness of peace which should characterize Christian community (3:15-17).

FOUNDATIONS.
3:1-4.

> **3** If then you have been raised with Christ, seek the things that are above, where Christ is, seated at the right hand of God. ²Set your minds on things that are above, not on things that are on earth. ³For you have died, and your life is hid with Christ in God. ⁴When Christ who is our life appears, then you also will appear with him in glory.

The fundamental principle for Pauline morality is that Christians are a dead and newly-risen people. Despite outward appearances, we are already raised to a new and higher life, interiorly but powerfully by God's grace. This grace had symbolic expression in the rite of baptism when the catechumen emerged from total immersion like a child emerging from the womb or like Christ emerging victorious from the tomb. Genuine christian re-birth consists of gift and call, in that order certainly yet in equal proportions. While granting us real communion with the crucified and risen Christ, it also demands of us a reformed life-style corresponding to this new status. "Raised with"—a single word in the Greek text—is characteristic of Paul's Christ-centred spirituality. All significant steps in life's pilgrimmage are "with" him, but especially the first step of initiation into the vital power of his dying and rising.

The Pauline ideal of the spiritual life is no static, quietist passivity, resting on the laurels of baptismal grace, but rather a continual quest for higher things. This quest aims at discovering and putting into practise the baptismal identity that is ours. It requires us to become (upon the level of desire and action) what we truly are (upon the level of grace). The seed of Christ-life within us can grow to pervade every aspect of our personality, elevating and totally renewing our existence already in this present world. That is the theory. But what should we be seeking? Can we concretely discern the "things that are above," which Paul proposes as our goal? Clearly, he is not recommending exaggerated ascetical posturings such as those already dismissed in chapter two. Further on (vv.12-17) some positive moral implications of this risen life will be explained in terms of prayer, love, patience and mutual help. For the present we learn the object of our quest only through the generic phrase "Where Christ is."

Our centre of desire should be lifted above all that is transitory, sensual and mundane. The heart must be turned towards the risen Lord, not enslaved by things on earth (v.2). This ideal, strongly reminiscent of our Lord's words "where your treasure is, there will your heart be also" (Mt 6:21), does carry its own ascetical implications but without any harsh rejection of innocent, everyday human pleasures. The proper balance can be found in the example of Christ, as well as in what Paul says elsewhere about freedom and moderation in using the good things of life (Rom 6:12-14; 12:6-13; 14:2-6; 1 Cor 9:24-27; 1 Tim 4:4).

For the present, christian life is "hid" (v.3). In order to appreciate the impact of this hiddenness, we need to resonate to the power of Paul's Christ-centred devotion, and share his conviction that life's meaning is transformed, purged and renewed by the redemptive grace of the Passion. "Hidden" life refers to a state of mind wherein Christ is the inward measure of our projects and desires, and where everything is referred through him to its ultimate source— the fatherly love of God. It does not mean any literal withdrawal from human relationships or responsibilities, into the sterile safety of an ivory tower. If those who are "hidden with Christ" find themselves sheltered from many superficial cares, it is not because the externals of life have changed but because they steer their course by a new compass. Material ambitions fall into proper perspective. Belief in eternal life counters our feverish human anxiety to wring the last ounce of satisfaction from the present moment. The source of our hope is "hidden" insofar as it cannot be appreciated by the non-believing world (Jn 14:17-19); even to the believer, the reality of grace and divine indwelling remains wrapped in mystery, half hidden from ourselves. "Tis we, 'tis our estranged faces that miss the many-splendored thing" (Francis Thompson).

The *denouement* will come when Christ our life returns in glory. With a brief but gleaming expression of the basic christian hope, Paul offers the perfect transition from fundamental principles to practical exhortation. We have something to look forward to, while undertaking the programme of self-conquest proposed in 3:5ff. There is here (v.4) both an end and a beginning. It heightens what has gone before, since our life is no longer simply "with" Christ, but is actually identified with him. The identification of Christ and life has a strong Johannine flavour (cf. Jn 1:4; 14:6), though Paul adds his own special emphasis upon community. Christ "*our* life," Lord and animator of his church, must be jointly shared by those united in the common bond of hope and love.

Personal hope is closely tied up with expectation of a great future event, when the splendour of inward grace will be revealed, not only to believers but also to people who now despise and reject the claims of faith. History moves forward towards a great culmination which will vindicate the truth of the Gospel. Christian hope is far from any kind of dumb fatalism, or from viewing life as an endless cycle of birth and decay. Its thrust is linear, purposeful, optimistic, being focussed upon the ultimate return of Christ as judge and king. Paul usually refers to this awaited return as

Parousia (advent), a word that implies a definite future
event which will bring all other events to their consummation. Here however he prefers the term *Phanerosis* (appearance) establishing a strong link between present and
future: A hidden splendour already exists which will later
be openly demonstrated to all the world. Believers whose
mortal lives are animated by his hidden presence will then
share in his unveiled "glory"—a word combining the ideas
of "light" and "life" and a supreme degree of joy.

Practical Advice

Having established the foundations of Christian moral
living, Paul can proceed to offer practical counsels upon
how that ideal is fulfilled. Without actually laying it down
as a philosophical principle that "every agent behaves
according to its nature," he sets out to trace some of the
behaviour-patterns of man-raised-with-Christ. His movement from doctrine to morals (or indicative to imperative)
is nowhere more striking than here, with the explicit
"therefore" at the point of transition.

The strength of the following passage consists in its
contrast of opposites, which is perhaps the most effective
way to clarify a moral or religious message. Much used in
preaching, this method forms part of the church's heritage
from ancient Israel (Ps 1:1-6; Is 1:16-20; Jer 31:31-33 etc)
and from our Lord himself (Mt 5:21-45; 25:33-46 etc). It is
especially beloved by Paul; remembering the shock of his
own conversion-experience, he expresses the implications
of christian faith in terms of sharp polarity to what has
preceded it. Hence his typical contrast between Darkness/
Life, Flesh/Spirit, Death/Life, Old Ways/New Ways.
Like immigrants into the land of faith, the baptized must
leave behind many of their former customs and adapt to the
way of life in their new surroundings. This process is here
conveyed under the symbol of changing one's clothes: The
sinful ways of the past are cast aside like rags, allowing
the believer to dress in the whole outfit of virtues proper
to the baptized.

THE OLD WAY AND THE NEW.
3:5-10.

> [5]Put to death therefore what is earthly in you: im-morality, impurity, passion, evil desire, and covetous-ness, which is idolatry. [6]On account of these the wrath of God is coming. [7]In these you once walked, when you lived in them. [8]But now put them all away: anger, wrath, malice, slander, and foul talk from your mouth. [9]Do not lie to one another, seeing that you have put off the old nature with its practices [10]and have put on the new nature, which is being renewed in knowledge after the image of its creator.

To let the spirit live, the earthly side of ourselves must die. This call for radical decision is clearly an extension of the baptismal reference (v.3), but shifting the mood from indicative to imperative. Although they have already "died" (sacramentally) to all past sinfulness, they must deliberately appropriate this dying process, at the level of personal choice and moral effort. This is another instance of Paul's realism. For while "ideally, their metamorphosis is instantaneous, and takes place at the moment of their baptism, existentially it is a long drawn out process" (Murphy-O'Connor). Regeneration of habits may have its starting-point in an experience of conversion, but the full achievement continues throughout life in a series of new decisions to die to one's sinful inclinations.

What must be set aside is first described globally as "What is earthly in you" (or "those parts of you which belong to the earth"). This refers not to the physical body as such, but to what is elsewhere called "the old man" (3:9), or "the flesh" (Rom 7:25; 2 Cor 1:17; Gal 5:19), or "the present age" (Rom 12:2; 1 Cor 2:6; Gal 1:4). Its sig-nificance is moral rather than material. It includes all those attitudes and behaviour-patterns that run contrary to God's influence, to prayer and to loving relationships with one's neighbour. Nowadays many might question the propriety of using "earth" and "flesh" in such a negative sense; yet some such symbols were needed to convey the dichotomy perceived by the early converts between their pagan past and their christian ideals. Without any philosophical contempt of the material body, they knew it as weak, vulnerable, subject to temptation, and therefore as an apt sign for what must be transformed by the powerful grace of Christ.

The short but emphatic catalogue of pagan faults (vv. 5-9), like similar Pauline lists elsewhere (Rom 1:29-31; Gal 5:19-21; 1 Cor 6:9-11), shows that he excluded certain kinds of conduct as incompatible with the christian vocation. While the vices named are not completely distinguishable from each other, they convey the various aspects of intemperance, mainly in relation to sexual indulgence. "Passion" here signifies the consent to be carried along by evil inclinations, and is the passive side of "evil desire." Even more severely than the dangers of misused sexuality, "covetousness" is branded with special vigour. This disorderly desire for material wealth, with disregard for the rights or needs of others, constitutes a dangerous form of idolatry. It clogs the attention of the heart, extinguishes man's desire for God (cf. Mt 6:24), and can even be regarded as the root of all evils (1 Tim 6:10). The list consists essentially of those two fundamental vices, impurity and greed, which "divide between them nearly the whole domain of human selfishness"(Lightfoot). We might at first be surprized to find Paul so casually attributing such behaviour to his Colossian readers, even in past tense. But in order to say that these converts had once lived and "walked" according to the catalogue of vices, he would need no special confession of their guilt. He simply took it as axiomatic that brute selfishness belonged to the general pagan life-style, and that only by God's grace was it possible to rise above this debased level.

Another of his axioms is that persistent sin draws down its own nemesis, which in true Hebrew tradition he describes as the "Wrath of God." Most of the references to this Wrath (Rom 2:5; 5:9; 1 Th 1:10) point to the future day of Judgment to come. In this instance (v.6) the present tense is used, but the meaning is still future, with overtones of imminent threat. However splendidly sinners may seem to prosper, they are heaping up disaster for themselves since God's justice is sure; on the contrary, by their conversion from the old ways, the Christians have escaped this spiral of destruction.

Another of Paul's contrasts is the temporal "Once" and "Now" (v.8) again with the underlying idea that through baptism "all is changed, changed utterly!" (W.B. Yeats). The "all" which belongs to the dead past is further specified by another enumeration of vices, this time with special emphasis upon what is divisive and anti-social.

The outworn rags that must be discarded are here portrayed in ugly terms: anger, wrath, malice, slander, lies (v.8-9). First, is "anger," that violent discontent with people and situations which so easily leads to quarreling and embitters the spirit. Its twin is "wrath," a more short-lived burst than anger but one that can inflict wounds of insult that are slow to heal. Also at the level of interior emotions we find "malice," a sinister delight in the misfortunes of others, often coupled with desire to sow dissension and mistrust. As the outward expression of these emotions, Paul lists some sins of speech—in each case the kind of thing which injures community and destroys mutual trust. If we were simply to substitute these vices with their opposite virtues, the passage requires of Christians that their speech be kind, decent and truthful, mirroring the disposition of brotherly love which is in their hearts. Still, the very fact that this list of vices appears at all obviously implies that Paul realized his readers were in need of such reminders. The pull of the old ways was still present, however high their new ideals.

He moves on to speak of renewal according to a new nature (v.10). The moral description of this new nature will follow shortly (3:12-17), but first its doctrinal basis is presented: It must reflect "the image of its creator." Obviously this derives from the Genesis creation-story (Gn 1:27), but its direct and immediate reference is to Christ, the one who is par excellence "image of the invisible God" (1:15) and who fulfils perfectly the creative purpose of God. Our text bears close resemblance to "Put ye on the Lord Jesus Christ" (Rom 13:14). This process of clothing oneself in the Christ-nature continues all through life, during which our nature is "being renewed" by spiritual growth until Christ be fully formed in us (Eph 4:13-16). The phrase "in knowledge" does not intend to limit our renewal to intellectual insights only, though it very probably contains a corrective to the pseudo-knowledge proffered by the Gnostics. Its reference is to that personal appreciation of God and of his will (1:9-10) which marks the mature Christian. Growth in Christ includes a developing spiritual knowledge of this kind.

Steadfastness and Spiritual Growth

Since the ethical section of our epistle urges the active cooperation of Christians in seeking renewal of spirit, perhaps we may here take a general look at what Paul says about development in spiritual life. On this point he merely suggests in Col 3:5-10 the point of view which is described more fully elsewhere, both in the major epistles (Romans, Galatians, 1 & 2 Corinthians) and those of the captivity (Eph, Col and Philippians). His basic principle is clear: to fully appropriate what Christ has given us is not the work of a moment, but the challenging task of a lifetime. This is his response to any who find the christian life tedious, have grown weary in well-doing (2 Th 3:13) or feel tempted to look elsewhere for more spiritual fulfilment than they have ever yet experienced in the Church.

Evidently, there were some at Colossae—as indeed within the community of believers in any age, including our own—who suffered from this dissatisfaction or malaise.

Having indulged excessive expectations for personal fulfilment in the short term, they found themselves drained of
enthusiasm, bored with the christian ethic and mistrusting
its capacity to rekindle their spirit. In such a state, one can
easily fall prey to the latest devotional wave, especially if
it claims secret knowledge, immediate results and the
promise of new spiritual experience. The danger of deeper
disillusionment may not be perceived until later, when
the vaunted remedies prove empty and the last stage is worse
than the first. Jeremiah's warning to the frustrated seekers
of innovation often goes unheeded: "My people have
forsaken me, the fountain of living waters, and hewed out
cisterns for themselves, broken cisterns that can hold no
water" (2:13). For true renewal, Paul echoes this great
prophecy, in pointing the people back to the living well-
spring, now recognized as Christ.

The apostle accepts, indeed he enthusiastically declares,
that we are right to seek the fulfilment of our deepest
hopes. His formula towards this is not to adopt some
esoteric cult or any spurious new asceticism, but to gain a
new appreciation of what we already possess. Submitting to
the "empty deceit" of the pseudo-ascetics would leave the
Colossians less prepared than ever for facing the perplexities
of life. Far from enriching them, it would rob them even of
the small measure of stability and peace they still retained.
Yet they do not need to fall into this trap. The key to
genuine spiritual growth is already within their grasp: In
Christ dwells all the fullness, and from him derives all the
wisdom, peace and contentment man will ever need. "That
is Paul's answer to every inadequate, dissatisfied, disap-
pointed, disillusioned and exhausted soul" (R.E. White:
In him the fullness, p. 82).

With characteristic paradox, he says to those who are
anxiously seeking something better: "you have come to
fullness of life in him" (2:10). This surprising assertion
comes within a context which implicitly urges development
to fuller maturity, both in knowledge and faithfulness

(1:6,9-11,23,28; 2:1-2,6-7,19; 3:1-2,10,12-17; 4:2-6). How can they be said to have "come to fullness" when there is obviously so much room for improvement? Firstly, because to be in contact with Christ is to be under the influence of God, since the fullness of deity dwells in him (2:9); to seek spiritual fulfilment apart from him would be a delusion. Secondly, because the baptized have received the grace of redemption, having been reconciled, forgiven and "made alive together with him" (1:20; 2:13). In principle, though in a way hidden from ourselves as well as from outsiders (3:3), we share already in the abundant life of Christ. All authentic spiritual development must build on this foundation, bringing to consciousness that hidden treasure implanted within us, and giving it expression in attitude and action. Whatever Paul may say elsewhere about the grim struggle between the spirit and the flesh, or between the old Adam and the new, his outlook is profoundly optimistic, since "where sin abounded, grace abounded all the more" (Rom 5:20). We already have the "first-fruits" and "pledge" (2 Cor 1:22; Eph 1:14) of that glory which will be revealed to us (Rom 8:18).

So much for the principle. There remains a great deal of practical effort to be made, in order to cooperate with this implanted grace and bear the fruits God expects from us. Paul shows a patient attention to detail, when outlining the way of christian virtue, repentance and renewal. In the first of his epistles, he urges us to walk as children of the daylight (1 Thes 5:8)—with peace, mutual help, efforts to do good, forgiveness, prayer, joy and thankfulness and an alert discernment between the various possible forms of good which preachers might propose (1 Thes 5:14-22). Typically, this encouragement is both buttressed and elevated by prayer: "may the Lord make you increase and abound in love to one another and to all men" (3:12)—since Paul may plant and Apollos may water, but it is God who grants the increase (1 Cor 3:6). In passing, there is something slightly curious about the use of agricultural imagery by Paul, the city man. His preferred metaphors were from urban life, the law-courts, market-place, arena, military parade, building-site, temple and town house; or from the human body itself, whose complexity mirrors the manifold unity of the Church. It may well be, as David M. Stanley suggested (*The Apostolic Church in the New Testament*, p. 363), that Paul's agrarian images derive from the parables of Jesus, as a means of teaching about the kingdom of God. At any rate, Paul shares with our Lord the style of beginning with the announcement of salvation, and then proceeding to clarify what this new age requires of disciples.

Undoubtedly, there is a problem created by this juxta-position of the indicative and the imperative; it often surfaces in the form of the (Protestant) challenge "are you saved?" answered by the (Catholic) admonition to "work out your salvation in fear and trembling" (Phil 2:12). Treating of the Pauline ethic, Rudolf Schnackenburg admits the "unmistakable tension between the certainty of salvation and the fear of not being saved" (*New Testament Theology Today*, p. 87). How can this tension be resolved, without abandoning either the radical rebirth wrought in baptism, *or* the challenge to continuing growth and renewal? The key lies in recognizing that Paul viewed salvation as "a word with three tenses: a past event, a present experience and a future hope" (A.M. Hunter: "Christianity according to St. Paul", in *Introducing New Testament Theology*, p. 91). Insofar as it depends upon the cross of Christ, and upon baptismal introduction to the community of faith, our salvation is *already* accomplished—implanted within us as a new seed of life. Yet our *present* experience mingles this conviction with a sorry history of sin and relapse: salva-tion must be worked out by God's help, in a world where the insidious pull of "the flesh" is also operative. It is here that we need detailed guidance such as Paul provides, upon the manner of life befitting a member of Christ's Body (Rm 12-15; Col 3-4 etc). Salvation is also a *future* blessing, insofar as it is the ultimate purpose of history, when Christ will appear (Col 3:4), and hand over the Kingdom to the Father (1 Cor 15:28). In this sense, we "await a Saviour" (Phil 3:20), by whom we "shall be saved" (Rom 5:9). During the period of waiting, we must live "sober, upright and godly lives in this world" (Titus 2:12) so that he will recognize us as his own (Mt 7:21-23; 25:11-13).

Within such eschatological expectation of the Lord's return, one could suspect that our moral efforts signify nothing more than simply "holding fast" to our identity, in a dour attitude of "no surrender." Like Jesus, Paul does indeed insist upon endurance where necessary, so that people will be "established in the faith" (Col 2:7), but like the Master he also insists that there is no faithfulness without attempting to make progress. This insight is particularly remarkable in the three great epistles of his captivity, as though the sight of prison walls had sharpened his awareness of spiritual growth through unity with the sufferings of Christ. So we find him desiring deeper union with the Lord "I press on to make it my own, because Christ Jesus has made me his own" (Phil 3:12); praying that his people may be "rooted and grounded in love, and have power to . . . know the love of Christ which surpasses knowledge" (Eph 3:17-19); and affirming that they must "hold fast to the Head, from whom the whole body . . . grows with a growth that is from God" (Col 2:19).

The key which explains why steadfastness and growth go together is precisely the indwelling Lord. Paul's own experience, from conversion to captivity, had shown him that loyalty to Jesus was a dynamic, not a static relationship. "Daily experience of life in the christian community, constant struggle to safeguard its truth, prayerful pondering of God's promises to Israel and persevering meditation on Christ's own words—all this taught Paul how dynamically the Lord is really living among his own" (Barnabas Ahern: *New Horizons*, p. 132). To people eager for spiritual novelty—whether at Colossae or elsewhere—the apostle's advice is: Go back, and discover the challenge, the promise

and the joy that are already ours in Christ. Only there can
be found the growth that comes from God.

"He is a path if any be misled;
He is a robe, if any naked be;
If any chance to hunger, he is bread;
For those who live in bondage, he is free.
    Whoever is but weak, in him finds strength;
    To dead men life he is, to sick men health;
    A treasure without loss, contentment beyond length;
    To blind men sight, and to the needy wealth."

G. Fletcher (quoted by White: *In Him the Fullness*, p. 86).

These lines nicely capture that blend of steadfastness and
renewal which characterizes the ethical appeal of St. Paul.

MANKIND REUNITED.
3:11.

> [11]Here there cannot be Greek and Jew, circumcised
> and uncircumcised, barbarian, Scythian, slave, free
> man, but Christ is all, and in all.

In this dawning age when people have imbibed the Christ-
life and are seeking the things above, the whole range of old
prejudices, castes and tribalisms that divide mankind must
give way before a new humanity, united and reconciled.
This marvellous vision does not at all involve the destruction of individual identity, as though each were to be simply
a carbon-copy of his neighbour, Paul's ideal for christian
community was marvellously pluralistic. It depended upon
each member placing his or her special gifts at the service
of the others, in a mutually advantageous harmony that enriched the whole group (Rom 12:4-8; 1 Cor 12:14-31; Eph
4:11-13). What must be destroyed are those divisive notions
of superiority and inferiority based on social, cultural
or religious grounds.

Some outstanding sources of discord will need to be overcome, to achieve this ideal. As in his earlier major statement on christian unity (Gal 3:28), Paul uses three pairs of contrasts to illustrate the divided condition of mankind. However, the Galatian text has a slightly wider scope than Col 3:11, placing the universal distinction "Male and Female" where our verse has "barbarian (and) Scythian," a narrower reference based on local interest rather than gender. The other two pairs of contrasts are virtually the same in both texts: Jew and Greek, slave and free.

A very deep alienation separated the devout Jew from those who followed the traditions and culture of Greece. Even where the two peoples lived cheek by jowl and where members from each had joined the christian community, seeds of the old hostility survived. Despite Paul's sustained campaign to establish liberty from the Mosaic law, and even after the sources of that plea at the Jerusalem meeting (Acts 15:19-20), some Judeo-Christians persisted in claiming superiority over their Gentile brethren on the basis of belonging also to the circumcised, covenanted heirs of Abraham and Moses (Gen 17:9-12; Ex 12:48). A hard-line minority of them still wished to impose circumcision as a condition upon all male Christians (Gal 5:6-12). Some remainder of this tension was obviously felt in the Colossian church also, where Jewish traditions were being foisted upon the community (2:16). The apostle counters this with renewed insistence upon the one thing necessary: belonging to Christ. Besides this, no special advantage is conferred either by the traditions of Moses or by the intellectual and aesthetic culture of the Greeks.

Just as the foreigner was religiously disdained by the Jew, so was he scorned on a cultural level by the Greek. "Barbarian" expresses this disdain in which all non-Greek-speakers were held, no matter how high a level of civilization they might have reached. Among the barbarians held in lowest esteem by the cultural elite at Colossae would be the wild mongol tribes of Scythia, that trackless wilderness lying north and east of the Black Sea. Yet, within the

Gospel of Christ, equal welcome was extended to the most backward tribesman as to the most erudite philosopher. Education and genuine culture may be highly prized within the church, but only when rooted in an affable spirit of courtesy and respect towards the unlearned.

The third division of society was still more iniquitous than the other two, and far more offensive to our modern liberal outlook. In Paul's day most people regarded the distinction of free citizen and captive slave as a normal and necessary state of affairs, dictated by war, tradition and the inequality of destiny. The apostle himself accepted this *status quo* as a social fact (cf. 3:22), but insists that on the deeper level of religious faith any such segregation is meaningless and must be transcended within the christian community.

Can these fissures be overcome, to achieve the reunion of Mankind? "Yes," answers the sublime faith of Paul. When Christ is finally recognized as the radiant centre of renewed humanity, and his universal lordship is truly welcomed, then all our shallow distinctions based on race, culture or social background will disappear before the tidal wave of brotherly love. Already his gospel has made important strides towards establishing unity and equality upon earth. "The idea of mankind as one family, children of the one God, is an idea of christian growth. Humanity is a word you look for in vain in Plato or in Aristotle" (Lightfoot). It is the particular merit of St. Paul to have so clearly linked this ideal of brotherhood with the major prospect of our faith, that the spirit of Christ must reign in our world.

VESTMENTS OF HARMONY.
3:12-14.

> [12]Put on then, as God's chosen ones, holy and beloved, compassion, kindness, lowliness, meekness, and patience, [13]forbearing one another and, if one has a complaint against another, forgiving each other; as the Lord

> has forgiven you, so you also must forgive. [14]And above
> all these put on love, which binds everything together
> in perfect harmony.

This appeal, among the loveliest in all Scripture, emerges
from the preceding with the powerful logic of a new day
dawning. Up to now the message has been to strip off the
tattered rags of hate and division. Now comes the moment
for dressing afresh, in the beautiful outfit of harmony.
Other notions will then be added to the basic "clothing"
image—peace must "rule" them and the word "dwell"
among them—providing a rich description of how a community will look when Christ is its vital centre.

The terms "chosen, holy and beloved" are instinct with
memories of the Old Testament, recalling Israel as a chosen
people (Ex 19:5) who shared in the sublime holiness of
Yahweh himself (Lev 19:2; Is 6:3) and were loved by him
not for their deserving but by his gracious choice (Deut 4:37;
7:7-9). In the era of the new covenant, that favoured status
once conferred on Abraham's descendants has been freely
granted to people of every nation through the church of
Christ, the new and universal Israel. After all that was said
earlier about the risen life and a renewed humanity, it
might indeed seem an anti-climax to speak instead of a new
Israel. But "the transition was a natural one for anyone
brought up on the Old Testament" (Caird). As used elsewhere by St. Paul, a common current of significance at-
taches to each of the epithets: "chosen," "holy," "beloved."
Together they constitute his powerful call to "live your
vocation" (cf. Eph 4:1-3), aspects of which he now proceeds
to name.

The virtues listed in v.12 have an obvious common
denominator, since all refer to interpersonal relations and
serve to highlight different facets of the manifold virtue
of love. Thus the list reinforces the ideal of community,
already so prominent in this epistle. Although the qualities
named require little explanation it may be useful to draw

attention to some points of detail. The one word "compassion" translates a phrase whose literal sense ("bowels of compassion") connotes tenderness of heart, a feeling of emotive sympathy for the distress of others. This was a virtue even more rare in St. Paul's day than in our own. "If there was one thing the ancient world needed, it was mercy . . . . The maimed and the sickly went to the wall; there was no provision for the aged; the treatment of the idiot and the simple-minded was unfeeling" (Barclay). It may be too much to say that Christianity brought mercy into this world—but the tiny glimmerings of compassion which were already there did receive an immense boost from the christian faith.

Kindness and lowliness complement each other to constitute the general "Christian temper of mind" (Lightfoot). A modest estimate of self, with the awareness of dependency upon God and of fitting into a scheme of things designed by Providence, prepare us for a benign approach to life. One who is God-centred rather than self-centred finds room in his heart to love all others whom God has made.

Meekness and patience would greatly facilitate the exercise of mutual forgiveness (v.13) which was quite essential for the survival of community life. The apostle's appeal for a patient and forgiving spirit (1 Cor 13:4; 2 Cor 2:7; Eph 4:32; Gal 5:22; Rom 15:1) confirms his reputation as a lucid realist regarding personal relations. Be they ever so devout, Christians would still occasionally get on each other's nerves. Their differences of opinion might even lead them betimes to such a heated quarrel as Paul himself had with Barnabas (Acts 15:39). Where disagreements could not be averted by patience or long-endurance, they must be repaired through meekness or "gentleness"—a quality of "willingness to make concessions" (Moule). Obviously what is here recommended is the very opposite to that wrathful anger belonging to "old nature," which—by baptism and in principle—Christians have already stripped off (vv.8-9).

As the Lord has forgiven you: Our most permanent and powerful motivation for mutual forgiveness is the divine mercy towards ourselves (v.13) which must then be reflected in our dealing with others. Several gospel texts connect the two, notably the Lord's prayer (Mt 6:12-15; Lk 11:4) and the parable of the unforgiving servant (Mt 18:32-35). In the parable, the master's initial gratuitous pardon is revoked when the servant proceeds to deal harshly with another: divine forgiveness is both cause and result; it follows as well as precedes the mutual reconciliation of disciples. This idea is probably implicit in vv.12-14, which indeed read like a summary form of the Matthean "community discourse" (Mt 18:15-35). "The Lord," whose mercy we must imitate, can refer either to the Father (cf. 2:13; Phil 1:29; Eph 4:32) or to Christ, whose "Lordship" is so prominent in Colossians. Significantly, the verb "to forgive" is closely related to the word for "grace" (*Charis*), both carrying overtones of abundant generosity in giving. The forgiveness required of a Christian is one very practical application of the Gospel axiom "freely you have received; freely give" (Mt 10:8).

Above all these they must put on love. Almost every descriptive list of virtues in the New Testament culminates in *agape*, that special brand of fraternal love which Jesus singled out as the very hallmark of discipleship (Jn 13:35). Like an all-enveloping cloak, it binds together the rest of one's spiritual clothing, just as it covers up a multitude of sins (1 Pt 4:8). Paul is not here suggesting that charity can exist in isolation from the other qualities mentioned up to this point, which are indeed its essential constituents (cf. 1 Cor 13). Yet there is a special warmth and depth in the christian experience of love that enriches and brings to completion every other effort one can make. In this sense, love is the "bond of perfection," a Hebraism for "the perfect binding," without which any other virtue can become lop-sided, disproportionate and empty (1 Cor 13:1-3). So central is this love to the whole gospel message that it can be suitably described as the complete fulfilment of christian law (Rom 13:10; Gal 5:14).

From this high ramp of reflection Paul can launch the luminous appeal of vv.15-17, which constitutes an inspiring nucleus for the epistle's moral section.

THE FULLNESS OF PEACE.
3:15-17.

Just as the first half of the epistle reaches its peak in the great hymn to Christ (1:15-20) so do these three verses stand out as the pinnacle of the second half. They show the positive face of morality in a most attractive light, totally alien to the harsh, judgmental spirit with which it can sometimes be confused. They present the christian ideal in terms of joyous, peaceful harmony among people whose concern for each other is no less real than their shared worship of God. Here too we see how Christ stands at the centre of the community's moral life as well as of their faith. Enveloped in his peace and guided by his word, they do all things in his name and direct their gratitude to the Father through him. It would be hard to find a fuller or more satisfying statement of his unique influence and mediation.

> [15]And let the peace of Christ rule in your hearts, to which indeed you were called in the one body. And be thankful. [16]Let the word of Christ dwell in you richly, as you teach and admonish one another in all wisdom, and as you sing psalms and hymns and spiritual songs with thankfulness in your hearts to God. [17]And whatever you do, in word or deed, do everything in the name of the Lord Jesus, giving thanks to God the Father through him.

The "Peace" of Christ is that inward security and contentment ("*Shalom*") which Israel had long awaited as the hallmark of the Messianic age, and which was now perceptibly present among the friends of Jesus. It was the Lord's personal legacy to his church, as John reports (Jn 14:27), and enjoys special prominence among the blessings Paul prayed upon his readers. In one text he actually calls Christ "our peace." But like the other gifts of God, peace had to be actively welcomed and practised by the recipient. It has that grace-quality of gift and call; granted as an inheritance, it is preserved through loyal exercise. Like the joy which is its twin, peace is an active not a passive element.

This peace must "rule" our hearts. The Greek verb which means literally to act as umpire or referee is a metaphor from the athletic arena, where decision must be given in favour of one or other competitor. Just as the umpire has the final word, so we should allow the powerful spirit of Christ's peace to arbitrate between our various desires. John Chrysostom comments: "He established for all disputes an interior arena, including contest, struggle and umpire . . . Do not let rage act as your umpire, nor contentiousness, nor merely human peace. For human peace is based merely on self-preservation and the avoidance of suffering." Christ's peace, on the other hand, disposes one to a more generous and reconciling attitude towards people and events.

Under his guidance, each disciple becomes a peacemaker, "eager to maintain the unity of the Spirit in the bond of peace" (Eph 4:3). Paul insists that this peaceful spirit belongs essentially to our vocation as people "called in the one body." His favourite description of the Church as the Body of Christ (1 Cor 12:12ff; Rom 12:5; Eph 1:23; 4:15) was already so well-known among the Christians of the Eastern Mediterranean that he could simply allude briefly to it and be confident of being understood even by a local church he had not yet visited. What a wealth of hope, challenge and consolation is here compressed within a single verse. At its foundation is the belief that the baptized have peace and thankfulness as their rightful inheritance, through membership in the living Body of the Lord.

Within the succinct phrase "be thankful," Paul captures a whole spiritual current of early Christianity. They were schooled by the apostles to be a grateful "eucharistic" people, highly conscious of the privilege of belonging to Christ through the mystery of divine election (Rom 1:8; 1 Cor 1:4; Eph 5:20 etc.) Where such gratitude ruled, quarrels could be submerged in the shared joy of being God's redeemed people. With the risen Christ as their living centre already radiating upon them the glow of the future life, their sense of thankfulness was intensely communitarian and led to a deeply shared worship of God (vv.16-17).

Verses 16-17 achieve a remarkable blending of doctrinal content with practical advice upon how to permeate the church's life with faith and fervour. Together, they illustrate the very finest ideal for prayer, both public and private. Verse 16 offers a brief glimpse into a christian assembly at prayer, and is followed by a sweeping invitation to extend worship into the whole of one's existence. It is a power-packed integration of liturgy and life. Without a sense of thankful worship in our weekday working existence, we have little to bring to our community's assembly for prayer. On the other hand, after taking an active part in that assembly, one's sense of God's blessing upon everyday life is heightened and renewed.

The "Indwelling Word" of Christ is capable of at least three meanings. It can mean the Lord's interior guidance of one's individual spirit; or it might refer to the remembered sayings of Jesus; or to the message *about* him as it was then preached within the assembly of Christians. In the light of what follows about mutual instruction, the third meaning is preferable. Indeed it incorporates the other two, since any true preaching centred on Christ must include the handing on of his remembered teaching, and thereby foster his continued guiding presence in the hearts of the hearers. The listening and believing church is the true home where this word can richly dwell. Not many years were to pass before that preached message reached its abiding written form in our four Gospels, which convey to future generations of believers what the spoken word of the apostles brought to the first generation. But in order to dwell richly among us, the written word of the gospel will always need the accompaniment of vital preaching and faithful acceptance within the church.

The members of a christian community have the right and duty of mutual admonition, in order to preserve a living faith and high moral standards among themselves. Paul would elsewhere single out particular individuals whose pastoral work he formally recognizes: Timothy, Tychicus, Epaphras and other "fellow-workers" (1:1; 4:7,12,17). But here there is no limitation of ministry to church officials; rather, the privilege and duty of fraternal encouragement is open to all. What is unclear (in the Greek text) is whether this mutual teaching should be qualified by the phrase "in all wisdom" (the *quality* of teaching) or by the "psalms, hymns and songs" (the *vehicle* or method used). While the latter sense could indeed be defended grammatically, it is hardly possible to limit mutual instruction within song alone. The former is the more likely meaning intended by Paul, especially since earlier he has prayed for their growth in wisdom (1:9). As community, they are to help one another to understand God's will and be faithful to it—for this is the heart of Christian wisdom.

The mention of psalms, hymns and songs (v.16) suggests that some kind of liturgical assembly is envisaged. From the very earliest days, hymn-singing featured within the Christian prayer-meeting, as part of our heritage from the Jews. Christ himself and his apostles sang a hymn at the conclusion of the Passover Supper, before going to the Garden of Olives (Mt 26:30; Mk 14:26). The custom continued within the apostolic church (Acts 4:24; 16:25; 1 Cor 14:26), as a joyful and meditative way of proclaiming faith. Outsiders could regard such singing as typical of the christian assembly: "They gather before dawn and sing together a hymn to Christ as to their God" (Pliny's letter to emperor Trajan, A.D. 112). Some rhythmic fragments within Paul's letters belong to this tradition of early hymns to Christ, notably Phil 2:5-11; Eph 5:14; 1 Tim 3:16 and of course the celebrated passage in Col 1:13-20. It is not unlikely that Paul wrote or adapted these strophes, to be sung by himself and the brethren.

At best, only a partial distinction can be sought between the hymns, psalms and spiritual songs. According to Gregory of Nyssa (4th century) "A psalm is a melody played by a musical instrument, a song is a musical utterance made with the mouth, and a hymn is the praise of God because of the good things we have received." While this gives a characteristic emphasis to each, one could well combine them into a song of praise, accompanied by an instrument. On the other hand, the psalms intended here would probably be those of David, still highly revered in the early church. The hymns would then be specifically christian compositions, based upon the gospel message. Both of these fall within the wider category of spiritual songs, but this might also extend to musical glossolalia or "singing in tongues," such as practised in recent times within the charismatic movement.

Thankfulness in the heart: It is not enough to go through the motions of prayer and mutual encouragement. These things—like everything else—must be done from the heart. The Greek text actually has the lovely phrase "singing in your hearts to God," an emphatic appeal for interior worship (cf. Eph 5:19). Significantly, the word "thankfulness" can also mean "grace." Appreciation and gratitude towards God are among the first and most precious fruits of his grace within our hearts. They render the faithful ready for proper participation in eucharistic community. They are also the necessary dispositions for those who wish to teach others the wise guidance and admonitions of the christian faith.

The momentum of this fine passage comes to a head in verse 17, with its exhortation to do all in the name of the Lord Jesus. This is a verse of great doctrinal and moral intensity, summing up the major insights of the whole epistle. As is usual with Paul, the doctrine firmly supports the moral guidance.

Doctrine: Paul's favourite description for Jesus is that of "Lord." To acknowledge Jesus as Lord became the central act of faith (Phil 2:11) empowered by the Holy Spirit (1 Cor 12:3). Already the Colossians have accepted this faith (2:6), even though it has been threatened by contamination from ideas alien to the full lordship of Christ (2:8-19). Essentially this "lordship" means not only that all good things originate "through" him, but that they are also "for" him. He is the mediator through whom things must be referred back to God, as well as having played a part in their creation (1:16). This conviction about the centrality of Christ which permeates the whole of the epistle is summed up here. Furthermore, the phrase "God *the* Father" (where Paul normally uses "God *and* Father") evokes the thought of Jesus' divine sonship, already prominent elsewhere (1:15; 1:19; 2:3).

Guidance: In practise, acknowledging Christ as Lord must express itself by a habitual attitude of referring to him in any and every situation, submitting our whole life and work to his influence. Such unconditional loyalty is capable of inspiring constant renewal of mind and outlook. As a test for any word or action, one may ask "Can we do it, calling upon the name of Jesus? Can we speak it and in the same breath name the name of Jesus?" (Barclay). Doing things in his name is such a power-packed notion. It reminds us of our belonging to him as members of his body, branches of his vine, empowered to act as his ambassadors in this world. It is seeking the things that are above (3:1) and living out the conviction that he is our life (3:3). Dominant quality of everything done in that name will be thankfulness, here repeated in the text. Gratitude to God, the most basic

religious attitude taught in the Scriptures both by word
and example, reaches its best expression when offered
through the mediating name of our Lord. This tradition
is well maintained in the liturgical prayers of the church,
but is meant to touch the furthest and most private corners
of our lives.

HOME AND FAMILY LIFE.
3:18 - 4:1.

After the elevated idealism of the preceding passage,
the next section which treats of domestic morality may
appear rather low-key and humdrum. It offers some
pragmatic advice on the working relationship which should
prevail beween man and wife, parents and children, masters
and slaves. Detailed ethical advice of this kind is found
in several other New Testament epistles (Eph 5:22-6:9; Titus
2:1-10; 1 Tim 5:9-16; 6:1-2; 1 Pt 2:13-3:7) and may be
termed "household instructions." It shows another side of
the apostolic preaching. Paul clearly realized that religion
cannot dwell forever on the peaks of mystical ideals and
universalist attitudes, but must be applied to the practical
circumstances in which people relate to one another.

From the beginning, detailed ethical guidance was found
to be helpful and necessary, and indeed must continue to be
given to the faithful in every age. Still we are bound to
enquire whether Paul's advice upon domestic matters is
truly applicable today, under modern social conditions.
Nowadays the subjection of wife to husband seems a highly
suspect demand, and institutionalized slavery has happily
long since vanished from the legal systems of the civilized
world. Even within Paul's own stated outlook there appears
to be some tension between these instructions and the
radical equality declared in 3:11 ("neither slave nor free")
or more dramatically in Gal 3:28 ("there is neither Jew nor
Greek, neither slave nor free man, neither male nor female;
for you are all one in Christ").

It would surely be mistaken to read this passage as a fixed immutable ethic, binding for all time upon the faithful. Paul's attitude to the Mosaic law and his sustained defence of Christian liberty would rule out any such interpretation. Rather, what he here offers is his considered advice as a pastor to his people within the social customs of the day, upon how to apply their faith to relationships within the home. There were many prototypes for this kind of instruction, both in late Judaism and in the ethics of Stoic philosophy. Jewish wisdom literature includes advice upon the training of children (Sirach 30), about choosing a wife (Sir 36:22-25) and an abundance of practical matters. Detailed instruction of this kind was also furnished by the Stoic moralists—one of whom, Seneca, a distinguished contemporary of St. Paul, refers to "that part of philosophy which gives advice suited to each individual without its being applicable to all, but shows the man how to behave towards his wife, the father how to train his children, the master how to control his slaves" (*Letters* 94:1).

Are there characteristics which distinguish Paul's ethical tenets from those of his Jewish and pagan contemporaries? There are in fact two: his emphasis upon mutuality, and his basic motivation of being true to Christ. Rather than focussing all the rights in one half of a relationship and all the duties in the other, as Roman and Jewish ethics tended to do, Paul takes into account also the husband's duty towards his wife, the parents' towards the children, and the master's towards his slave. His deeply-held principle of brotherhood and of equality in God's sight demanded this kind of reciprocity; and in this way the requirements of the gospel filtered through into social relationships within the early Church.

Secondly, the motivation for harmony within the family derives from their fidelity to Christ. Belonging to him, they must act appropriately, whether at home or in the larger assembly of the local church. Hence the remarkably frequent reference to the Lord (five times within the space of six verses) which connect this family advice with the great principle in v.17 ("all in the name of the Lord Jesus"). The dominant interest of this passage is not its social conservatism, but rather "that household life was so transformed in the Lord that each person was seen as precious to God, and that husbands and masters recognized that they had duties as well as rights" (Moule).

> [18]Wives, be subject to your husbands, as is fitting in the Lord. [19]Husbands, love your wives, and do not be harsh with them. [20]Children, obey your parents in everything, for this pleases the Lord. [21]Fathers, do not provoke your children, lest they become discouraged. [22]Slaves, obey in everything those who are your earthly masters, not with eye service, as men-pleasers, but in singleness of heart, fearing the Lord. [23]Whatever your task, work heartily, as serving the Lord and not men, [24]knowing that from the Lord you will receive the inheritance as your reward; you are serving the Lord Christ. [25]For the wrong-doer will be paid back for the wrong he has done, and there is no partiality.
>
> **4**   Masters, treat your slaves justly and fairly, knowing that you also have a Master in heaven.

Wives and Husbands

A spirit of docile obedience on the part of the wife, problematic though it may sound to modern egalitarian and emancipated ears, would have seemed to Paul a necessary domestic virtue in order to keep peace within a family. He regarded the husband's authority in the household not as an artificial social convention favouring the male but as a God-given dictate of nature, a view more fully expressed in 1 Cor 11:3 and Eph 5:23. Yet such authority and docility needed the counterpoise of love and respect; without love, the obedience would be hollow and the authority could have nothing to do with Christ. Elsewhere, too, the apostle suggests the good influence that could be had by a docile

wife over her pagan husband (1 Cor 7:12-16), as an example
of virtue strengthened by faith. But while one may understand his reasons, both doctrinal and practical, for offering
this advice, one finds it difficult today to say with conviction "Wives, be subject to your husbands." We must at
least set it within the context of broader principles such as
"bear ye one another's burdens" (Gal 6:2) and "be subject
to one another, out of reverence for Christ" (Eph 5:21).
An important corrective is already supplied in v.19 requiring husbands to love their wives. In effect, this signifies
partnership in the marriage-alliance, and rules out that
"harshness" or domineering spirit which could so easily
result from a one-sided stress on obedience. Each of the
partners is called to a generous spirit, the very opposite
of self-centredness. "If a wife is asked to submit, it is to her
husband's love, not to his tyranny" (Moule).

Children and Parents

If the Christian ethic holds firm to the fourth commandment as given through Moses (Mt 15:4; 19:19), it balances
this with the reciprocal obligation of parents to be gentle
and considerate with their children. Paul is emphatic upon
the duty of children to obey, but adds two qualifications
to show that such obedience enshrines a religious value.
First, the child is told to obey its parents in everything,
not merely in those disciplinary matters needed for the
peaceful running of a household—mealtimes, cleanliness
and the like. One would have to make exceptions to such
absolute docility, of course, at the level of individual
cases: where parents make unreasonable demands of an
adolescent, or abuse their parental authority. But the
command is stated in this positive form, as a guiding
principle for those households where a good and healthy
spirit prevails. Secondly, this is reinforced by the motive
that it "pleases the Lord"—surely an echo of the blessing
attached to the fourth commandment "that it may go well

with you in the land which the Lord your God will give you"
(Deut 5:16). Implicit is the idea that, in submitting to the
loving guidance of parents, the child is really accepting
the mediated guidance of God. Absent from our text,
however, is any explicit mention of growth towards auton-
omy, though some element of this may fairly be discerned
in the following verse.

To counter any danger of authoritarianism whereby
parents could crush the spirit or stifle the spontaneity
of their children, Paul adds the gentle counsel "do not
provoke them." This is a far cry from the harsh discipline
of "Spare the rod and spoil the child" enjoined by Jewish
wisdom (Prov 13:24; Sirach 30:7-13). Its purpose may
include the protection of youngsters in the Colossian
community from the ascetic rigours already mentioned
(2:18). In general, this verse breathes a mature tolerance
for youthful high spirits and *joie-de-vivre*. Children must
be allowed enough free play and be given enough parental
approval to grow confident in their own abilities and
develop an optimistic disposition towards life. A steady
diet of corrections and restrictions, without any clear
demonstration of love, would make it virtually impossible
for the child to understand the prayer "Our Father." Paul's
counsel, on the other hand, keeps a nice balance between
the essential roles of parenthood: instruction and affection
(cf. Eph 6:1-3). Their blending offers the child his or her
best hope of positive education, in the Christian sense.

Masters and Slaves

The five verses 3:22-4:1, which are closely paralleled
elsewhere in the New Testament (Eph 6:5-9; 1 Tim 6:1;
Titus 2:9-10; 1 Pt 2:18) show that the early church accepted
the institution of slavery, in practise at least even if not in
fundamental principle. The problem this raises has already
been mentioned, and will be more fully discussed later.
First we should notice how Paul attempts to humanize and

baptize this unjust institution. He reminds slaves of their human dignity and spiritual potential, and warns slave-masters of the ultimate judgment of a just God. To the extent of his power, but without going into the philosophical or anthropological roots of the practise, he tempers slavery with the gospel.

Obedience is enjoined upon slaves, while at the same time their dignity is protected in several ways, primarily by means of the contrast between the earthly and the heavenly master. For those who accept Jesus as ultimate Lord of one's life, the significance of an immediate superior is relativized. Doing the imposed task need not be humiliating, since a positive motive (to please the Lord) lifts the situation above one of fearful servility. The only fear proper to a Christian, slave or free, is reverential "fear of the Lord"—the willing acceptance of God's providential will in our lives. The point is three times made that all service is ultimately to the Lord. Hence the encouragement to "singleness of heart" in their work, a spirit that would drive out the cringing reluctance so typical of slavery. A second support of their dignity is the prospect of divine reward for work well done. The "inheritance" of life within God's Kingdom belongs equally to all believers, and depends upon faith and fidelity, not on position in the social wheel. While he was among the disinherited of this world, the slave could look forward in hope towards a better future and this hope sustained his sense of personal worth here and now. Thirdly, Paul insists that the slave take responsibility for his own actions: no less than the free man, he would be punished by God for his sins. This was a necessary corrective to the temptation of total irresponsibility which easily attracts those whose freedom is diminished. It is good to be reminded that, in a profound sense, we are masters of our own destiny no matter what the external circumstances in which we live. The advice in verse 23 echoes verse 17, and applies to all believers whether slave or free.

Finally, the impartial justice of God is directed towards the ruling class as their motive for fair dealing with those who serve them. In harmony with the rest of the ethical section, the fundamental order to be oberved is not merely one of social convention but rather one which will please the Lord who judges hearts. It is not enough for Christian masters to stay within the civil law, since this gave them almost limitless rights in their treatment of slaves. A higher law must prevail: the will of Christ, our "Master in heaven," whose words about brotherly love apply to the relationship between master and slave. In modern parlance, this verse demands attention from employers, investors and foremen of every kind. Its relevance has not diminished even with the happy disappearance of slavery but continues wherever there is a clash of interest between the powerful and the weak.

Why did Paul not condemn slavery outright?

We might well wonder why the first Christian preachers did not draw the logical social conclusions from their religious message, and roundly attack the unequal state of society in their day. But before blaming Paul and his colleagues for conniving at injustice, we need to remember several factors influencing them and try to understand their priorities:

a) From time immemorial, slavery had featured as an institution within the Jewish as well as the Gentile world. It was easier to consider it in terms of greater or lesser harshness than to plan its total and radical abolition. Paul's message tended towards substantial humanization of the relationship between masters and slaves.

b) The Roman empire provided a golden opportunity for the spread of the gospel, so long as Christians were not perceived as lawless revolutionaries, intent on over-throwing the established order. Hence they avoided open conflict until it was forced upon them; they appealed to the current law (Acts 22:26; 25:12) and maintained the duty of civil obedience (Rom 13:1; Titus 3:1).

c) Jesus, by rejecting the path of violent revolution had given the guideline of cooperation within the social and political system while maintaining the primacy of a kingdom not of this world (Jn 18:36-37).

d) Paul's priority throughout was the spread of the faith, expecting the early return of Christ in judgment. In view of the imminent prospect of entry into the vision of God, the burden of social inequalities would have appeared secondary to him, and something to be patiently borne, in hope.

PRAYER, ZEAL AND PRUDENCE.
4:2-6.

Paul turns again from specifically domestic ethics to the wider community of the faithful, and rounds off his moral advice with two brief appeals applicable to them all. Zealous for the spread of the gospel, they must be constant in prayer and thoughtful in their dealings with their pagan fellow-citizens. Both of these counsels reflect the practical wisdom of one who knew human nature and its foibles very well. Much earlier he urged his readers to pray constantly, to encourage and strengthen one another (1 Thes 5:11,17), for one could so easily grow "weary in well-doing" (2 Thes 3:13). Another, very different temptation was that of rash enthusiasm, arising from an excessive confidence in Spirit-guidance, whereby the charismatic believer could ignore all human opinion, especially that of the outside observer (1 Cor 14:23). This would be a misleading, arrogant spirituality, and one harmful to the spread of the church. Authentic zeal needs the twin supports of petitionary prayer and common prudence.

PRAYER AND ZEAL.

[2]Continue steadfastly in prayer, being watchful in it with thanksgiving; [3]and pray for us also, that God

may open to us a door for the word, to declare the mystery of Christ, on account of which I am in prison, ⁴that I may make it clear, as I ought to speak.

Here the emphasis is upon petitionary request, even though an underlying spirit of thanksgiving can never be absent. We must continue to acknowledge our needs before God, and in the process we receive increase of power to do his blessed will. Steadfast and alert—these dual qualities were the standard advice of the apostolic church in regard to the true prayerful spirit. Jesus himself in the Garden of Gethsemane had bidden his companions "watch and pray" (Mk 14:38 and parallels), and the same requirement was very soon applied to all Christian disciples (1 Th 5:6; 1 Cor 16:13; Eph 6:18; 1 Pt 5:8; Rev 3:3). The watchfulness mentioned in v.2 has no obvious connection with expectation of the Lord's imminent return, and is almost synonymous with steadfastness. But possibly it contains also "a vivid flash of reminiscence of the literal sleep which Paul has heard about in the story of the Passion (Mt 26:40) or of the Transfiguration (Lk 9:32). It means being vigilant as opposed to lethargic while at prayer" (Moule).

They pray a blessing upon his apostolate. It is highly significant that the special intention here recommended aims at the spread of Christ's message rather than any personal convenience for the apostle himself. Prisoner though he was, growing old, and no doubt somewhat burdened by ill-health (cf. 2 Cor 12:7; Col 1:24), Paul might well be excused for some appeal for their sympathy, or their prayers for his release. Yet the concern of his heart is outward-looking, seeking an opening for further apostolic activity. The word—the saving message of the gospel— came first. Beyond the door of his prison cell, Paul dreamed of other open doors, of hearts open to receive the gospel and respond to it with faith. Only God could unbar those doors, and smooth the way for his messengers to proclaim his word. He had done so in the past (cf. 1 Cor 16:9; 2 Cor

2:12), and would do so again if his people were earnest in their asking. Through intercessory prayer, the opening of new opportunities for the word could begin even while Paul was still in prison, if only he can find the right technique to present and make it clear to others. Here is no complacent cleric, content to repeat old time-worn formulae, without regard to their suitability for the particular audience facing him here and now. The true apostle is zealous to find the right verbal and emotional key to fit the door of those hearts, should God present him opportunity to speak.

In a paradox typical of his style, Paul states that what he must make clear to all is nothing less than God's most profound secret, the mystery of Christ. Already we have seen this contrast at 1:26, where it is more fully explained. The point here is that this great revelation (the love of the Father, given through his Son) requires to be preached by these fragile human instruments God has chosen, if it is to illumine the many hearts for which it is destined. Men like Paul are needed to make this mystery known. Yet it was precisely for publicizing it that he now finds himself imprisoned! Though he works in mysterious ways, our heavenly Father must be constantly petitioned to open new paths for the preaching of his Son's saving passion and resurrection.

PRUDENCE AND ZEAL.

> [5]Conduct yourselves wisely toward outsiders, making the most of the time. [6]Let your speech always be gracious, seasoned with salt, so that you may know how you ought to answer every one.

Paul urges prudence as well as zeal towards the non-church public (vv.5-6). Where Christians are only a tiny minority-group within a pagan population, they stand in particular need of a good external relations policy. This was the case with all of the Pauline churches, as with many a missionary group today. The advice given by the apostle is twofold: "Conduct yourselves wisely" and "make full use of the time"—a nice balance of prudence and zeal that would help keep the peace while spreading the faith.

Considering his own great drive in missionary work, it is obvious that Paul wished his readers also to avail of every opportunity to share their faith with others. Just as Jesus would have us be salt and light to the surrounding world, so Paul bids us regard every moment as a privileged opportunity for bearing witness. He uses the same notion of "harvesting" the precious passing moment in Eph 5:16, with the added comment that "the days are evil." The disciple redeemed by Christ must in turn redeem the times in which he lives, influencing others by the example of a Christ-like life and not only by the verbal preaching of his gospel. This demands a kind of holy opportunism so that we "buy up the entire stock of opportunity" (Moule), letting slip none of the chances we are given of furthering the spread of faith and love. This kind of apostolic involvement is the right and duty of every adult Christian, according to Paul.

On the other hand, an insensitive zeal for preaching the gospel can be, unhappily, counter-productive. A tactless, monotonous or uninvited harangue will neither help to recommend one's faith nor win the hearer towards conversion of outlook. To gain a sympathetic hearing from outsiders we must first have their respect (1 Th 4:12), and then try to assess what is the most opportune way of sharing our vision with them. In this sense, prudence becomes the essential ally of zeal. There will be a time to speak and time for silence, dictated as much by the other's mood as by one's own. Furthermore, a gracious pattern of speech, salted with a seasoning of wit, is the best vehicle for speaking about Christ. "The Christian must commend his message with the charm and wit which were in Jesus himself" (Barclay).

This sensitive, adaptable prudence does not contradict but helps to counterbalance, Paul's insistence elsewhere upon avoiding merely human wisdom when preaching the Cross of Christ (1 Cor 1:18-2:5). Each one must, to the extent of his or her possibilities, become "all things to all men" (1 Cor 9:22). In this sense the lay apostle no less than the cleric must try to gauge "how to answer every one." Different kinds of people need different approaches. It is up to us to be aware of the other's background, feelings and ideals, before attempting to lead him further in the direction of God. Without a real attempt at sympathetic under- standing it may be well to stay silent, for "the greatest disservice that can be done to the gospel is to make it seem insipid" (Caird) or irrelevant to the human concerns of our fellow-citizens today.

With these injunctions upon prayer, zeal and prudence Paul brings the moral section of his epistle to a suitable conclusion. It then remains for him formally to introduce the bearer of the epistle, and add a list of personal greetings intermingled with admonitions.

IV Encouragement and Farewell (4:7-18)

This final section of the epistle is devoted to greetings to various men and women known to Paul and his friends. Since it consists to a large extent in a roster of names, one might at first be tempted to ignore these, expecting no relevant message from them. On a closer inspection how- ever, the list of friends turns up many an interesting detail, and the whole spirit of this passage is redolent of the epistle's central theme: unity in Christ.

What could be more normal to find at the end of a letter than a list of personal greetings from friends to friends. Paul is no exception to this custom. If there is anything remarkable in his letter-endings it is the sheer number of people he mentions, indicating the wide range of his friendships and his keen recollection of individual personalities. In this regard, these eleven verses bear comparison with the final chapter of Romans, with its listing of numerous friends, all of them acquainted with the people receiving the letter. While this section does not open up any doctrinal or moral instruction, it deserves attention for two reasons: the attractive light it casts upon Paul's human relationships, and the inspiring parade of his friends to whom he introduces us. The cross-section of personalities conjured up here would be typical of the first generation of gentile Christians, our forefathers in faith. "Heroes of the faith," one author calls them, though he tends to over-dramatise their perils—"Remember the circumstances: it is always dangerous to be a prisoner's friend, for it is easy for the friend of the prisoner to become involved in the same fate as the prisoner himself. It took courage to declare oneself a friend of Paul, and to show that one was on the the same side" (Barclay). There is no need to suppose that all or even most of them stood in grave danger of persecution from the Roman authorities. At any rate they were a small but admirable minority-group within a pagan world, and their spirit has much to teach us today, in an increasingly "Diaspora" situation.

THE BEARERS OF THE LETTER.
4:7-9.

> [7]Tychicus will tell you all about my affairs; he is a beloved brother and faithful minister and fellow servant in the Lord. [8]I have sent him to you for this very purpose, that you may know how we are and that he may encourage your hearts, [9]and with him Onesimus, the faithful and beloved brother, who is one of yourselves. They will tell you of everything that has taken place here.

Tychicus was a Christian from proconsular Asia, possibly from Ephesus (2 Tim 4:12), known to Paul for some time, at least since accompanying him on the voyage from Macedonia to Jerusalem (Acts 20:4). He knows all about the apostle, having visited him in his (Roman) prison, and can be entrusted with letters both to Colossae and Ephesus (Eph 6:21). Along with delivering the written message— which as we've seen is highly compressed with doctrine and exhortation—he could add his own remarks about Paul's activities and state of health, just as he would also to the Ephesians (6:21-22). This factor helps to explain the absence of everyday chronicle or gossipy elements in the epistles.

As well as delivering the letter and passing on other news by word of mouth, Tychicus will also "encourage your hearts"—a gracious description for that edifying task which any apostolic visitor must perform. He is held in high esteem by Paul, as shown by the triple description "beloved brother," "faithful minister" and "fellow-servant," phrases conveying that lively sense of partnership which marked the apostle's whole approach to ministry. Apart from his mission to Colossae he acted as Paul's delegate on several other occasions (2 Tim 4:12; Titus 3:12). It is doubtful, however, whether one would be justified in regarding him as Paul's personal "deacon" even though the combination of "minister and fellow-servant" very soon came to apply specifically to the relationship of deacon to bishop, in the letters of Ignatius of Antioch (Ephes 2; Magnes 2; Philad. 4).

Onesimus: We know him from elsewhere as a runaway slave who, upon turning Christian under the influence of Paul was then sent back to his master, Philemon, himself also a Pauline convert. Our text suggests that the home of both slave and master was at Colossae, since Onesimus is to take his place in the local community as "one of themselves" (spiritually as well as geographically). It is interesting that the word "slave" or servant is not used here of this man. His position of social inferiority does not in any way prevent him being accepted as a "faithful and beloved brother," capable of sharing in the Christian apostolate. In ways like this, rather than by a frontal assault upon the prevailing legal system, the apostolic church both mitigated and undermined the evil of slavery.

GREETINGS FROM SEVERAL FRIENDS.
4:10-14.

> [10]Aristarchus my fellow prisoner greets you, and Mark the cousin of Barnabas (concerning whom you have received instructions—if he comes to you, receive him), [11]and Jesus who is called Justus. These are the only men of the circumcision among my fellow workers for the kingdom of God, and they have been a comfort to me. [12]Epaphras, who is one of yourselves, a servant of Christ Jesus, greets you, always remembering you earnestly in his prayers, that you may stand mature and fully assured in all the will of God. [13]For I bear him witness that he has worked hard for you and for those in Laodicea and in Hierapolis. [14]Luke the beloved physician and Demas greet you.

Aristarchus: A Macedonian from Thessalonika, (Acts 20:4) one of the first towns evangelized in Europe (Acts 17:1). He probably received the faith from Paul himself, then proceeded to prove himself a true friend, sharing Paul's journeys and dangers—to the point of being seized during the riot of the silversmiths in Ephesus (Acts 19:29), and continuing with the apostle on his voyage of imprisonment to Rome (Acts 27:2). Paul describes him as "fellow-prisoner," a term which could signify spiritual captivity (i.e. as slave to Christ), but whose more likely reference is to sharing in physical imprisonment. If so, we do not know for what reason Aristarchus was jailed, unless he had voluntarily accompanied the now elderly apostle into house-arrest at Rome, in order to be of service and act as messenger. It could be, indeed, that his friendship with

Paul in Rome had aroused suspicion and led to a brief jail-sentence (Lightfoot). Elsewhere the same term "fellow-prisoner" is used of others: Epaphras (Philem 23), Andronicus and Junias (Rom 16:7). Possibly a rota of good Christian friends contrived to keep Paul company during his various imprisonments! At any rate, an impression of fellowship and interdependence is uppermost here.

Mark, the cousin of Barnabas: This brief mention of the two cousins who had shared in Paul's first missionary venture is particularly interesting, since it implies that a heart-warming reconciliation has taken place. Barnabas, "the son of consolation" (Acts 4:36) appears as one of the most popular personalities in the apostolic age. He had gained Paul entry into the Jerusalem community and later into that of Antioch (Acts 9:27; 11:26). Along with his (young?) cousin, John Mark, he sailed with Paul to Cyprus on the first great mission (Acts 13:5), but soon Mark left them and returned to Jerusalem (Acts 13:13)—back to the home comforts of his mother's house (Acts 12:12). Angry with this desertion, Paul refused to allow John Mark join in his next preaching journey, thus provoking a quarrel with Barnabas, after which they parted company (Acts 15:36-40). Some years later we find Paul's positive appreciation of Barnabas as a hard-working man (1 Cor 9:6), but also a mild criticism of his indecision (Gal 2:13). And when here, for the first time, he speaks of Mark, it is in terms of friendly courtesy: "make him welcome." By now, Mark has been completely reinstated as a valued "fellow-worker" in the spread of the gospel (Philem 24). If only all discord between Christians could be so happily resolved! A further word of praise for Mark is added in 2 Tim 4:11 where his service to Paul is "very useful."

Other important items traditionally associated with Mark are that he served as assistant and "son" to St. Peter (1 Pt 5:13); that he wrote a gospel in Rome, for the Romans (Irenaeus 3,1,1), and that he was for a time bishop of Alexandria in Egypt (Eusebius, H.E. 2.16—not a very reliable account).

Jesus Justus: This is the first and only time he appears in the New Testament. Probably he was "not a man of any prominence in the Church, but his personal devotion to the Apostle prompted this honourable mention" (Light- foot). Both his names are typically Jewish, the first being a derivative of "Joshua" (Yahweh saves) and very popular in our Lord's time, the other signifying "just" or God fearing, signifying his devotion to the Mosaic Law (cf. Acts 1:23 and 18:7 for two early converts having that name). Paul adds the remark that only these three, of the whole Jewish- Christian group at Rome, associate themselves with him in working for the kingdom of God. This need not mean that the Christian Jews had no apostolate of their own, but simply that they held aloof from Paul's version of the gospel. Perhaps they resented what they considered to be his abandonment of the Law and his defence of gentile liberty. Or it may be that they were still suspicious of one whose conversion was so dramatic, from zealous persecutor to ardent propagator. For his part, Paul made several efforts to allay the fears of his Jewish-Christian brethren, col- lecting relief-funds on their behalf (1 Cor 16:1-4; 2 Cor 8-9), going in devout pilgrimage to Jerusalem (Acts 21:26) and being careful in his statements about the precious Jewish heritage (Rom 7:7; 9:4-5). So perhaps he does not mean that literally "only" these three men remained friendly towards him, but rather that only they were prominent in working with and for him. They were a particular comfort, helping him to bear the sorrows of exile and imprisonment, insofar as they were from his own national and religious background.

Epaphras, on the other hand, provided another kind of consolation, since he embodied the whole throng of Gentile converts whom Paul had won for Christ. We have already met him as Paul's beloved companion (1:7); he now emerges as "one of yourselves," i.e. a native; or at least a one-time inhabitant of Colossae. Since this was the man whose report on their progress had prompted the writing of the epistle, Paul hastens to commend him for the good work he had done among them before his journey to Rome—and

among the faithful at Laodicea and Hierapolis too, since the
three communities were in regular contact with each other.
Now, at a distance from his people, Epaphras continues
"struggling" on their behalf—the same struggle of persevering prayer and petition in which Paul himself engages
(2:1; cf. Rom 15:30). The special concern of both men is that
the little community will stand fast in the faith, thus at-
taining genuine maturity of the kind God wills (and not
any spurious kind of growth, such as that by the pseudo-
philosophers of 2:8-23).

Luke, The Beloved Physician: Here is another of Paul's
closest friends, one upon whom the New Testament gives
various hints which were later developed by Patristic
explanations, and later still woven into Taylor Caldwell's
full-length novelistic portrayal "Dear and glorious
Physician." His name is the shortened form of Lucanus,
quite common in the Roman world, and before his conversion he had been a pagan, not a Jew (4:11). A very early
tradition identified him with the author of the third Gospel,
and of Acts (Irenaeus 3.14.1). This may be why certain
portions of Paul's journeys are reported in the first-person
plural, as by a friend and eye-witness (Acts 16:10-18; 20:7-
21:17; 27:1ff). It has been suggested that Luke joined up
with Paul during the second mission at a time when the
apostle was troubled with some physical ailment (Gal
4:13) and needed medical aid. If so, then we owe as much to
his physician's skill, which maintained Paul in health as we
do to his literary art which has given us some of the most
beautiful writing in the New Testament. He was beloved
to Paul, not only as physician but also as "fellow-worker"
(Philem 24), committed to spreading the christian message.
There is further the suggestion—if we may rely on 2 Tim
4:11—that he shared in Paul's final imprisonment, (whether
as a prisoner himself or as a regular visitor), a true friend
for all seasons!

Other, less reliable traditions concerning Luke would
identify him with Lucius of Cyrene, one of the group of

prophets and teachers in the church at Antioch (Acts 13:1), and regard him as a painter who left behind him several icon-portraits of our Blessed Lady.

GREETING TO SEVERAL OTHERS.
4:15-17.

> ¹⁵Give my greetings to the brethren at Laodicea, and to Nympha and the church in her house. ¹⁶And when this letter has been read among you, have it read also in the church of the Laodiceans; and see that you read also the letter from Laodicea. ¹⁷And say to Archippus, "See that you fulfil the ministry which you have received in the Lord."

Nympha and the Church in her House. Among the faithful at Laodicea, Paul singles out this woman—though the Greek name might as easily be that of a man—along with her christian family and friends. Though the Church is worldwide, its roots are in the local and domestic communion of believers, and there is no clear evidence of separate buildings set apart for worship until the third century. In those early days, the primary meaning for "church" was wherever two or three were gathered in Christ's name (Mt 18:20), as here or in the house of Priscilla and Aquila at Rome (Rom 16:5).

The Letter from Laodicea: Paul's instructions upon the reading of his letters suggest several points. First, he is emphatic that all the Christians at Colossae should hear what he has written to them; there must be no attempt at suppression of his warnings, by those who might find them uncongenial—similar precaution is taken in 1 Thes 5:27. Then they may read a further expression of his thought in a letter to be collected from the faithful at Laodicea. If this letter is not (as Marcion held it to be) identical with what we now call Ephesians, then it appears to have been lost, since there is little basis for identifying it with the letter to Philemon (J. Know: *Philemon among the letters of Paul*).

The Ministry of Archippus: This interesting instruction shows that Archippus, called a "fellow-soldier" or comrade-in-arms (Philem 2) held a significant role of leadership in the church at Colossae (or at Laodicea, possibly), and that the community members were to encourage him to fulfil it well. This seems both an implicit rebuke to Archippus (for failure to defend the Gospel with sufficient vigour against the heretical trend) and an attempt to strengthen his ministerial authority for the immediate future. His ministry has been "received"—quite possibly from Paul himself, since the term used "suggests a mediate rather than a direct reception" (Lightfoot)—'in Christ," that is ultimately under the Lord's direction and for the good of the Church, Christ's people. Paul clearly recognized the need for clear and acknowledged leadership in each local church; this brief admonition has parallels elsewhere (1 Thes 5:12; Phil 1:1; Eph 4:11), and prepares the way for a much fuller treatment of formal ministry, in the Pastoral Epistles.

FAREWELL SIGNATURE.
4:18.

> [18]I, Paul, write this greeting with my own hand. Remember my fetters. Grace be with you.

Whereas the text of his letters was dictated through a secretary or scribe (like Tertius, Rom 16:22) Paul would append his signature and a few last words of greeting in his own untidy hand (Gal 6:11; 1 Cor 16:21; Philem 19). This was not only to close the letter on a personal note, but also to authenticate it as genuinely coming from him (2 Thes 2:2; 3:17). Indeed, his signature probably appeared even on those epistles which do not draw specific attention to that fact.

Mention of his fetters occurs at the end, not as an appeal for sympathy but to further establish the significance of the epistle, as though to say "these chains are God's guarantee of my sincerity and my apostolate." It is a theme used with great effect in Eph 4:1 and Phil 1:14. Apostolic imprisonment is the most powerful witness, for "he who is suffering for Christ has the right to speak on his behalf" (Murphy-O'Connor). Such a man, enduring on behalf of the Church (1:24), carries conviction in praying the grace of God upon his readers! And so the letter ends upon the same positive, encouraging note with which it began.

Colossians – A Challenge for Today

Reading this epistle attentively, not merely as an interesting document from antiquity but as part of our basic heritage from the inspired apostolic age, we will have noticed many points relevant to our present situation, touching us both as private individuals and members of christian communities. Paul's vigorous words will challenge us, as they did the original readers, to reappreciate and confirm our full christian faith. In view of particular thought-currents in today's world, this epistle can help us re-gain our balance regarding christology, firm moral principles and true spiritual growth.

(a) The unique status of Christ: The clear doctrine about Christ which we have inherited through Scripture and Creed stands in some danger today of being superseded or submerged within the medley of new attempts to expound his significance. Various factors can contribute to this: desire to return to a so-called simple or primitive "christology from below," emphasizing only the humanity and human limitations of Jesus, and the "servant" vocabulary that was used of him; an urge to recognize the values inherent in all the religious strands of our pluralistic social and religious milieu; reluctance to allow excessive weight to any doctrinal formulation from the past, however central or venerable; a search for new, thought-provoking

and existentially valid ways of expressing our faith. Each of these motives is in itself good, but together they can enkindle a threat to orthodox faith markedly similar to that against which Paul warns. How easily today's eclectic and liberal Christian can seek a compromise between Christ, Buddha, Krishna and Karl Marx. Modern equivalents to the elemental spirits of the universe would not be far to seek, packaged in the same beguiling speech which once threatened to hide the unique splendour of Christ. To such a trend Colossians says: "In him are hid all the treasures of wisdom and knowledge".... In him the fullness of deity dwells bodily . . . Through him God reconciled all things to himself."

Paul's attitude to the syncretist equating of Christ as just one among many mediators of divine power, was a resounding "No." Flexible though he tried to be, accommodating himself in manners, thought and vocabulary to the needs of both Jew and Gentile, he could tolerate no compromise upon the divine status and unique redemptive role of Our Lord. Yet it is worth noting how the challenge drew from him his highest and finest statement of christological faith. In this, rather than in anathema or threat, he found the most effective defence of the faith.

(b) Firm Moral Principles: One of the widespread ideals of our modern democratic (Western) world is tolerance towards value-systems differing from our own—and this is surely an advance from bygone centuries of feudalism and absolutism. This development is not an unmixed good however; it can often be but a short step from toleration to a lazy and spineless neutrality, reluctant to commit oneself to any strong moral values (such as the permanence of marriage or the inviolability of human life before birth). It may well be that many of today's nominal Christians, confused by conflicting lobbies either for the lightening or loosening of civil laws related to ethics, find themselves drifting into moral relativism bordering on indifference.

These will need the stimulus of Paul's virbrant call to "seek the things that are above," and live the life of a reconciled people "holy and blameless and irreproachable." Very positive principles of morality are declared, in regard to compassion, harmony, prayerfulness and gracious speech; while a wide range of activitites (3:5-11) is branded as incompatible with a truly converted christian life.

But if Paul promotes firmness in moral values, he rejects that stern rigorism which some would wish to impose under the banner of wisdom and good order. In the post-Conciliar Catholic Church, some voices appeal for a return to Tridentine discipline as an antidote to modern laxity. They would do well to notice the advice (Col 2:16ff) against passing judgment upon others in regard to externals of food, drink or festival—and perhaps of conventional clothing or uniform too. The most fundamental moral principle of all, throughout the epistle, is to hold firm to Christ, living and rooted and built up in him. Whatever is compatible with this "holding firm" will be free for Christians to use and enjoy. Paul's message is neither fussy, nor narrow, but promotes purity of intention (3:22-23) and interior peace.

(c) Spiritual Growth: In his reflections on the dynamic element in the Church, Karl Rahner observed that church officials usually find it easier to formulate general principles which are doctrinally true than to find specific policy initiatives which will be spiritually fruitful for the life-experience of ordinary people. Yet the faithful always require encouragement and guidance at the practical level too. Aware that their everyday life is a continuous process of change and development, we need to be shown avenues of growth in insight, faith and love, if we are not to remain stunted in the spiritual life. Paul insists that conversion is only the start of a long development. There remains a whole process of "clothing" in virtue to be gone through (3:12), and increased understanding and strength to be

gained, new fruits of good work to be produced, even though we already have redemption and forgiveness of sins.

What we must grow towards is "maturity" of a special kind, that of adult and interior conformity to Christ (1:28). But in working towards this goal we are not abandoned to our own unaided efforts: true growth in the spirit comes from God, as a vital force given to every member of the body of Christ (2:19). The conviction that all the baptized share a common vocation to holiness, and that their spiritual growth depends primarily upon the Holy Spirit's impulse is happily widespread in the Church today. But how many would equally appreciate that they also need a deeper spirit of endurance and patience with joy (1:11)?

In Colossians, the role of pastoral leadership within the church emerges in a very edifying and demanding light. A local pastor must listen to his people bidding him fulfil his ministry towards them (4:17). Communication appears as mutual dialogue, not monologue or diatribe. A vital part of the apostolate will be loving concern on behalf of the community; this is expressed by prayer, and even by ministerial suffering "filling up what is lacking . . ." (1:24). The pattern set by Paul for bishops and priests achieves an ideal blend of authority and loving sacrifice, a style of devoted leadership capable of providing persuasive guidance unmixed with any taint of authoritarianism. Thus he shows in practice how to produce the best context for spiritual maturation and to safeguard love "which is the bond of perfection" (3:14).

Considering its relative brevity, I am sure that this epistle contains a remarkable wealth of significance for ourselves, today. If our hearts are struck by its challenge and by its encouragement we will have advanced in no small measure towards the final fulfilment "when Christ who is our life appears" (3:4).

SUGGESTIONS FOR FURTHER READING

Since many commentaries include Colossians with one or more of Paul's other epistles, I have indicated after the publication-date of each volume listed the number of pages devoted specifically to our epistle. Most of the titles given are at a semi-popular level, though several technical works are also mentioned for those who require more detailed information.

William Barclay: *Letters to Philippians, Colossians, Thessalonians* (Edinburgh, St. Andrew Press, 1960; 97pp).
   A homiletic commentary laced with imagery and anecdote in Barclay's inimitable fashion. Occasionally capricious in its dramatization, yet always highly readable.

G.B. Caird: *Paul's letters from prison* (New Clarendon Bible; Oxford University Press, 1976; 57pp).
   Succinct commentary based on the RSV. Sparing but effective use of Greek terms. Good cross-references to related New Testament texts. Generally clear exposition, but sometimes excessively laconic.

J. Llewelen Davies: *The Epistles of St. Paul to the Ephesians, the Colossians and Philemon* (London, Macmillan, 1862; 45pp).
   An old-fashioned and very spare commentary on the Greek text, but with good introductory material on the spirit and style of the epistle. Makes a curious connection between the Colossian heresy and the Zoroastrian creed of ancient Persia.

Charles J. Ellicott: *St. Paul's Epistles to the Philippians, the Colossians and Philemon* (London, Longman & Green, 1865).

> Careful, ponderous, attentive to the textual evidence especially of the old Syriac versions; offers detailed explanations wherever there is ambiguity in the Greek text.

Joseph Grassi: *St. Paul's Letter to the Colossians* (Jerome Biblical Comm.; London, Chapman; New Jersey, Prentice Hall, 1968; 6pp).

> Compresses a remarkable quantity of information into six tightly printed pages. More useful as an aid to revision than as an introduction.

William Hendriksen: *A Commentary on Colossians and Philemon* (London, The Banner of Truth Trust, 1971; 205pp).

> Detailed and devout commentary, earnestly Protestant in parts. Sees an ominous parallel between the Colossian heresy and modern ecumenism. Otherwise quite helpful and readable.

John B. Lightfoot: *St. Paul's Epistle to the Colossians and to Philemon* (London, Macmillan; Grand Rapids, Zondervan; 300pp).

> A commentator's commentary, based on the Greek text; full of erudite background material from ancient authors and Patristic writings. Succeeds in combining this with a clear explanation of Paul's thought with particular emphasis on the various possible meanings for ambiguous phrases.

Ralph P. Martin: *Colossians – The Church's Lord and the Christian's Liberty* (Exeter, Paternoster Press, 1972; 164pp).

> Sub-titled "An expository commentary with a present-day application," this well-written book performs a function similar to that envisaged by the present series. Includes a good bibliography.

Eduard Lohse: *Die Briefe an die Kilosser und Philemon* (Meyer's NTComm.; Gottingen, Vanderhoeck & Ruprecht, 1968; 257pp).

> A modern rival to Lightfoot's monumental work. Scholarly, with up-to-date bibliography (20 pp) including items written in English up to the mid-60's. Maintains that Colossians was written in the post-Pauline generation.

Charles F.D. Moule: *The Epistles to the Colossians and to Philemon* (Cambridge Greek Testament Commentary; University Press, 1955; 94pp).

> Solid, medium-length commentary based on the Greek. Wears its erudition lightly. Good exposition of the theological content of the epistle. Useful bibliographical matter from periodical literature.

Harold K. Moulton: *Colossians, Philemon and Ephesians* (London, Epworth Press, 1963; 62pp).

> A preacher's commentary, lively and brief, with constant attention to the homiletic message of each section.

Jerome Murphy-O'Connor: *Colossians* (Scripture Discussion Comm., vol. 11; London, Sheed & Ward, 1971; 53pp).

> Lucid and lively portrayal of Paul's thought in an existentialist key, emphasizing the need of personal decision as pre-requisite for re-born existence. Bible-groups will appreciate the stimulating questions posed at the end of each chapter, underlining modern questions to which Paul supplies some answer.

Franz Mussner: *The Epistle to the Colossians* (New Testament for Spiritual Reading 17; London, Sheed & Ward, 1971; 93pp).

> Non-technical, medium-length commentary, expounding the spiritual meaning of each passage by reference to other portions of the New Testament.

A.S. Peake: *The Epistle of Paul to the Colossians* (Expositor's Greek Testament, vol. 3; London, Hodder & Stoughton, 1903; 70pp).

> Readable introduction, followed by a rather dull commentary—much of it grammatical—upon the Greek text.

E.F. Scott: *The Epistles of Paul to the Colossians, to Philemon and to the Ephesians* (Moffat's New Testament Commentaries; London, Hodder & Stoughton, 1930; 91pp).

> Medium-length and quite readable, but undistinguished.

G.H.P. Thompson: *The Letters of Paul to the Ephesians, the Colossians and Philemon* (Cambridge Bible Commentary; University Press, 1967; 70pp).

Based on the New English Bible text, this brief commentary is very well written, with many felicitous turns of expression and useful thematic material at the beginning and end.

Reginald White: *In Him the Fullness—Homiletic Studies in Paul's Epistle to the Colossians* (London, Pickering & Inglis, 1973; 155pp).

Maintains that the great difficulty about the message of Colossians is that "most of us assent to it without really believing it" (p.151) and makes an enthusiastic effort to remedy this. Highly readable.